## EDITORIAL

Editor: Allan Burney
(allan.burney@keypublishing.com)
Author: Tony Holmes
Designer: Philip Hempell
(phil@hempdesign.co.uk)
Artist: Russell Smith
(www.russellsmithart.com)

## KEY PUBLISHING

Managing Director: Adrian Cox
Executive Chairman: Richard Cox
Commercial Director: Ann Saundry
Marketing Manager: Martin Steele

© Key Publishing Ltd 2014
Key Publishing Ltd, Units 1-4 Gwash Way Industrial
Estate, Ryhall Road, Stamford PE9 1XP

Tel: +44 (0)1780 755131
www.keypublishing.com

Printing: Warners (Midlands) plc

Distribution: Seymour Distribution Ltd

ISBN: 978-1-910415-01-6

# CONTENTS

Painting by Russell Smith

AVIATION CAME OF AGE in the 1914-18 war. When the first shots of the conflict
rang out, flying machines were still regarded as nothing more than flimsy novelties. However
Commanders soon learnt that he who controls the skies, controls the battlefield... and the fighter
aircraft was born. Within four years, aircraft had evolved into battle-hardened killing machines.
Ace pilots were portrayed as modern knights, the dogfights as chivalrous duels. The face of
warfare had been changed forever. This is that story...

Arranged in chronological sequence, we look at the top 10 fighter aircraft of the conflict, their
evolution, combat history and the aces that flew them. From Fokker to Sopwith, from Manfred
von Richthofen to Albert Ball, this 100th anniversary special edition pays tribute to them all.

# A HISTORY OF CONFLICT
# BRITAIN AT WAR

As the UK's best selling military history title, Britain at War is dedicated to exploring every aspect of Britain's involvement in conflicts from the turn of the 20TH century through to modern day.

## BRITAIN AT WAR FEATURES:

**All the latest news and discoveries from around the UK**

**Features and analysis on major historical events**

**Conflict captured through photography in 'Camera at War'**

**Personal accounts from those involved**

**Reviews on the latest DVD and book releases**

AND MUCH MORE!

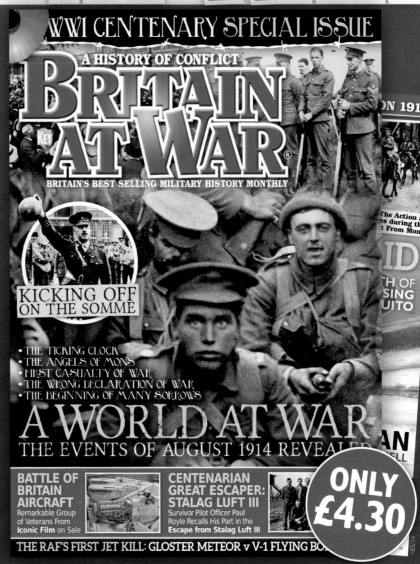

WW1 CENTENARY SPECIAL ISSUE

A HISTORY OF CONFLICT

## BRITAIN AT WAR

BRITAIN'S BEST SELLING MILITARY HISTORY MONTHLY

KICKING OFF ON THE SOMME

- THE TICKING CLOCK
- THE ANGELS OF MONS
- FIRST CASUALTY OF WAR
- THE WRONG DECLARATION OF WAR
- THE BEGINNING OF MANY SORROWS

## A WORLD AT WAR
THE EVENTS OF AUGUST 1914 REVEALED

**BATTLE OF BRITAIN AIRCRAFT** Remarkable Group of Veterans From Iconic Film on Sale

**CENTENARIAN GREAT ESCAPER: STALAG LUFT III** Survivor Pilot Officer Paul Royle Recalls His Part in the Escape from Stalag Luft III

ONLY £4.30

THE RAF'S FIRST JET KILL: GLOSTER METEOR v V-1 FLYING BO

Requirements for app: registered iTunes account on Apple iPhone 3G, 3GS, 4S, 5, iPod Touch or iPad 1, 2 or 3. Internet connection required for initial download.
Published by Key Publishing Ltd. The entire contents of these titles are © copyright 2014. All rights reserved. App prices subject to change. 551/14

# FOKKER EINDECKER

THE FOKKER EINDECKER (monoplane) truly started the age of fighter aviation, Dutchman Anthony Fokker fitting his scouts of 1915-16 with pioneering gun interrupter gear that enabled pilots to fire a machine gun directly ahead between the blades of the revolving propeller. The Eindecker duly caused consternation in the ranks of Allied airmen as its pilots began to reap a grim harvest of victims in 1915. The exploits of aces like Max Immelmann and Oswald Boelcke became legendary on both sides of the front. However, the Eindecker's reign over the Western Front lasted less than a year, as by early 1916 German pilots were finding it hard to handle the DH2, FE2b and Nieuport 11 biplanes now being fielded by the Allies. The 'lone hunters' of 1915 were largely gone as well, their place having been taken by airmen who flew together in new formations – the Jagdstaffeln.

**Widely regarded as the first true fighter aircraft, the Fokker Eindecker was the scourge of Allied pilots in 1915/16.**
*via AirTeamImages.com*

nthony fokker was born in the Netherlands East Indies on 6 April 1890, the son of a coffee exporter. Fokker moved to Germany in 1910 in an attempt to find employment in the budding aviation industry through a combination of his commercial and mechanical talents. By December of that same year an aeroplane of his own design – the Spin ('spider') – was ready for testing. By 1913 the entrepreneurial Fokker had established a factory at Schwerin and was producing aircraft for civil and military use.

To remain at the forefront of aviation's rapidly advancing business, Fokker obtained the latest French Morane-Saulnier H shoulder-winged monoplane and hired Martin Kreuzer as his chief engineer. Although the resulting M.5 single-seat Eindecker (monoplane) that emerged seemed to mimic the Morane-Saulnier's basic configuration, it differed from the wood-framed French aeroplane in having a structure that, aside from the wings, consisted of wire-braced chrome-molybdenum steel tubing with welded joints. Judging the Morane-Saulnier's rectangular rudder inadequate, Fokker replaced it with a comma-shaped control surface, which became a Fokker trademark for the next three years.

The M.5L was ultimately adopted by the German Fliegertruppe (air service) as the A.III and used in a so-called 'cavalry scout' role, gathering aerial intelligence in quick flights over the front. It was not long before competing airmen began taking pot-shots at one another with pistols, carbines, rifles, machine guns and even cannon. However, the history of aerial warfare was about to be changed forever by a revolutionary new invention — a machine gun that could fire throught a rotating propeller.

Since 15 July 1913, Franz Schneider of the Luftverkehrsgesellschaft (LVG) had held a patent for using a series of cams and rods attached to the trigger bar to interrupt the machine gun's fire whenever the propeller was in its way. Fokker, spurred on by wartime stimulus, worked up a means of putting the theories into practice.

After testing at Döberitz on 19-20 May, the German High Command was impressed enough to order five machine gun-equipped A.IIIs and M.5Ks (designated M.5KMGs and bearing the serial numbers E 1/15 to E 5/15), followed on 28 August by a production order for 36 E.Is, as the armed monoplanes were redesignated. The first armed product of Fokker's Schwerin factory, A.III A16/15, was issued in July to Ltn Otto Parschau of FFA 62 at Douai aerodrome. In a letter to Fokker on 28 July, Parschau complained that its Parabellum LMG14 incessantly jammed after a few shots, but noted that other Fokkers using the Spandau-produced Maxim LMG 08 performed excellently. Fokker quickly exchanged weapons accordingly.

The first Fokker to bear the Eindecker designation (E.I 5/15) was issued to Ltn Kurt Wintgens serving in Bavarian unit FFA 6b. He duly claimed a Morane-Saulnier L east of Lunéville on 1 July 1915. Because there were no witnesses to confirm the aeroplane's demise behind French lines, the first German fighter victory remained unofficial.

Meanwhile, in June, two more members of FFA 62 were given the opportunity to fly the E.I in combat. Both were friends, both hailed from Saxony, both harboured aggressive spirits suited for flying fighters and both saw the future of aerial warfare in the Fokker. There the commonality ended, however, for while 24-year-old Ltn d R Max Immelmann was almost a year older than Ltn Oswald Boelcke, the former was self-centred, arrogant and accused by one of his instructors as having 'a truly childish temperament'. Boelcke professed to be a loner by nature, but was more socially outgoing and mature than Immelmann.

In their new E.Is, Boelcke and Immelmann quickly began wreaking havoc on Allied reconnaissance aeroplanes.

**Oblt Kurt Student (left) relaxes in front of his Fokker Eindecker. These aeroplanes were all assigned to the Fokkerstaffel attached to the 3 Armee at Leffincourt.**
*via Author*

## THE FOKKER MONOPLANES

embodied a curious mix of the visionary and reactionary that characterised Anthony Fokker himself, and the German air service, throughout the war. In Fokker's case, at least, one can find an explanation for the paradox – inventive though he could be, he was first and foremost a businessman. Even while he experimented with new structures and devices, his practical

process of the armed Eindeckers that the E.III was replacing the E.II on the Fokker production line in September 1915. With 268 built for the German army, 14 additional units produced for the navy and 18 for export to Austria-Hungary and Turkey, the E.III was the principal variant to see action and the real source of the term 'Fokker Scourge' as its numbers proliferated along the front.

> ## 'THE ENGLISH RECONNAISSANCE TWO-SEATERS TREAT MY SINGLE-SEATER EINDECKER WITH A HOLY RESPECT' Ltn Oswald Boelcke

application of them was ultimately aimed at selling aeroplanes to Idflieg.

During the course of early Eindecker production Fokker did some minor refining of his basic formula, leading at first to the E.II (M14). This replaced the 80hp Oberursel U 0 rotary engine with a nine-cylinder 100hp U 1. Although some 30 percent more powerful and more reliable than its precursor, the engine was also larger and heavier, necessitating a lengthened fuselage and relocation of the cockpit and wings.

Fokker made little distinction between the E.I and E.II on the production line, recording a collective total of 85 before the E.III replaced them both. Both scouts had their 98-litre main fuel tank and oil tank located in front of the pilot, where the installation of the machine gun led to their having to compete for space with ammunition and the interrupter gear.

The only major difference between the Fokker E.II and the E.III was that the latter featured a new petrol tank aft of the cockpit and a modified front reserve tank that freed up more space under the cowling for the ammunition arrangement. Otherwise, E.IIIs and the five last E.IIs in the second production batch were indistinguishable. So swift was the refining

Fokker was determined to maintain the Eindecker's edge against any new opposition the Allies might devise. The resulting Fokker M.15, or E.IV, was powered by essentially two Oberursel U 0 rotary engines bolted together to produce a 14-cylinder double row version with an output of 160hp. In anticipation of the vibration the motor might also produce, support bearings were added to the engine mounts, extending to the front. To compensate for the engine's weight, the fuselage was enlarged to 24ft 8in (7.5m) and the height increased to 9ft 2in (2.75m). Armament on the E.IV was increased to two 7.92mm LMG 08 machine guns in the upper cowl, with an improved ammunition feed system.

Although faster in level flight and stronger and more heavily armed than its predecessors, the Fokker E.IV also proved to be less manoeuvrable and its engine less reliable. For one thing, the aft row of cylinders could not get as much cooling air as the front row, making it prone to overheating. Over time performance deteriorated, especially rate-of-climb and control responsiveness.

A total of 49 Fokker E IVs had been produced by March 1916, before an order for 20 more was cancelled in April.

# FROM THE COCKPIT

Wearing a balaclava, headscarf and fur-lined flying overalls, an unidentified German fighter pilot poses for the camera prior to taking off in his well-worn Fokker E.II. *via Aviation-images.com*

**ALTHOUGH THE FIRST** effective fighter to be sent aloft thanks to its unique armament, the Eindecker was not an exceptional aircraft in terms of its performance. Indeed, the machine's controls, which were not harmonised at all, demanded constant attention from the pilot. While the elevator and rudder were very light and required only the slightest movement of the control column and rudder bar – according to future ace Ltn Kurt Wintgens *'without any effort you can steer with two fingers'* – the wing warping was quite heavy.

A British pilot who flew the captured E.II E.210/16 noted that the lateral control was *'not good'* and the fore-and-aft control was *'distinctively bad'*. An official report on the aircraft by the RFC concluded that although the flying and engine controls were well placed in the cockpit, the Eindecker was laterally,

longitudinally and directionally unstable. It also noted that the aircraft was tiring to fly 'in any but still air'.

The ultimate Fokker Eindecker, the E.IV was easily the hardest of the breed to handle in the air thanks to the increased torque of its twin-row U III engine. According to Lt Otto Parschau, in climbing turns with full power a considerable amount of physical effort was required to operate the wing warping, and tight turns had to be helped by 'blipping' (cutting) the engine. The inertial and gyroscopic forces of the heavy U III rotary also made the E.IV less manoeuvrable. Franz Immelmann, brother of Max, was unimpressed with the E.IV: '*It was practically a flying engine. As long as it did its duty and rotated itself and its propeller, it imparted some unique flying qualities to the machine. The slightest trouble and any consequent irregularity in the engine's revolutions made it necessary for the pilot to switch off his engine and abandon his flight because the machine became virtually uncontrollable when the engine lost any of its efficiency*'.

## KNIGHTS OF THE AIR

### Max Immelmann

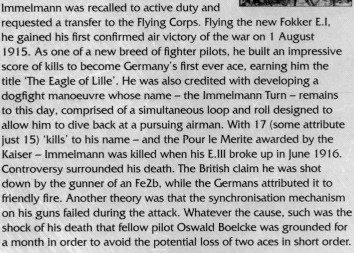

Max Immelmann was born in South Africa but chose to renounce his British nationality while studying medicine in Germany. Having joined the German Army he resigned his commission in 1912 in order to work as an engineer.

With the outbreak of war in August 1914, Immelmann was recalled to active duty and requested a transfer to the Flying Corps. Flying the new Fokker E.I, he gained his first confirmed air victory of the war on 1 August 1915. As one of a new breed of fighter pilots, he built an impressive score of kills to become Germany's first ever ace, earning him the title 'The Eagle of Lille'. He was also credited with developing a dogfight manoeuvre whose name – the Immelmann Turn – remains to this day, comprised of a simultaneous loop and roll designed to allow him to dive back at a pursuing airman. With 17 (some attribute just 15) 'kills' to his name – and the Pour le Merite awarded by the Kaiser – Immelmann was killed when his E.III broke up in June 1916. Controversy surrounded his death. The British claim he was shot down by the gunner of an Fe2b, while the Germans attributed it to friendly fire. Another theory was that the synchronisation mechanism on his guns failed during the attack. Whatever the cause, such was the shock of his death that fellow pilot Oswald Boelcke was grounded for a month in order to avoid the potential loss of two aces in short order.

# CONSTRUCTION

## FUSELAGE

The aircraft's fuselage skeleton was comprised of a steel-tube, square-section structure devoid of lugs or sockets. At the very front was the engine plate, and the engine was overhung from this. The fuselage tapered to a horizontal knife-edge at the tail, and it was fabric-covered. The semi-circular engine cowling and the forward-fuselage top-decking and side panels were sheet aluminium.

## COCKPIT

The pilot sat in a steel-tube framed bucket seat that could be slid along its bearers. Engine instrumentation consisted of a Morrel revolution counter, a pulsometer gauge and a pressure gauge. The aeroplane instruments were a fuel gauge and a compass.

## TAIL

The circular balanced rudder had a fabric-covered welded tubular steel frame, and had a balance area forward of the single vertical member that formed its axis of rotation. The elevator was of similar construction.

## WINGS

The 32ft 11.6in wings were two-spar wooden structures with no dihedral or sweepback. Lacking ailerons or flaps, the Eindecker relied on 'wing warping' for roll control and a balanced elevator for pitch control.

## ARMAMENT

The most-used armament on the Eindecker was the Spandau-produced 7.92 mm LMG 08 (which in the E.III had a 500-round ammunition belt), using the mechanical push rod interrupter gear devised by Anthony Fokker and his design team. The E.IV was supposed to boast three LMG 08s, but mainly flew with two. By late 1916 the push rod system had been rendered obsolete by the introduction of an improved electrical system, adapted to fit the 7.92 mm LMG 08/15.

## UNDERCARRIAGE

The main undercarriage was formed around the lower bracing pylon, each wheel being attached at the apex of a pyramid of three tubes. The bungee shock absorbers were housed inside the fuselage at the top of the outermost front strut. The non-swivelling tailskid was fitted with a knife-edge to keep the aircraft straight on landing.

## ENGINE

The E.I was powered by the Oberursel U O rotary engine, which was a licence-built version of the French Gnome seven-cylinder 80hp motor. The E.II and III were fitted with the improved nine-cylinder 100hp U I while the E.IV had the twin row U III of 160 hp installed.

### 1913

**July:**
Swiss-born engineer Franz Schneider patents his concept of interrupter gear for a forward-firing aerial machine gun.

### 1915

**June:**
Fokker E.Is, incorporating a variation on Schneider's interrupter gear developed by Anthony Fokker and Heinrich Lübbe, start arriving at Feldflieger Abteilungen (field aviation units) along the Western Front.

**1 July:**
Ltn Kurt Wintgens claims the Fokker E. first victo but it is n confirme

IN CLOSE-UP

The Spandau-produced 7.92mm LMG 08 machine gun dominates the view forward from the cockpit of the Eindecker. The effectiveness of this weapon is what gave the Fokker control of the skies over the Western Front in 1915-16.
via Aviation-images.com

## 1916

**ugust:**
Max
elmann is
ited with
2c for the
official
ory in a
ker E.I.

**11 January:**
In the first multiple grouping of fighters in the German Fliegertruppe (air service), Kommando Vaux, commanded by Oblt Rudolf Berthold, fields five Fokker monoplanes, operating under the direct command of 2. Armee headquarters.

**10 March:**
Oblt Oswald Boelcke arrives at Jametz aerodrome and subsequently moves up to Sivry to establish his own frontline response unit.

**28 June:**
Oblt Boelcke is credited with his 19th victory from the previous evening, then departs Sivry for the Balkans and Turkey – but not before writing his fighter tactics down on paper, to be distributed to German units all over the front.

**10 August:**
Oblt Hermann von der Lieth-Thomsen orders the formation of Jagdstaffeln, permanent fighter units ideally equipped with 14 fighters

**25 September:**
Ltn Kurt Wintgens of Jasta 1, still flying his Fokker E.IV because it mounts twin machine guns, is shot down and killed over Villers-Carbonnel by Lt Alfred Heurteaux flying a SPAD VII of N3

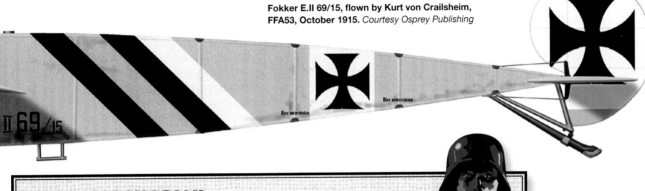

**Fokker E.II 69/15, flown by Kurt von Crailsheim, FFA53, October 1915.** *Courtesy Osprey Publishing*

## DID YOU KNOW?

- The Eindecker's revolutionary gun synchronisation gear was based on a system patented by Swiss engineer Franz Schneider of LVG, who in 1916 opened proceedings against Fokker for patent infringement. The courtroom battles continued until 1933, with the court's consistently ruling in Schneider's favour but Fokker adamantly refusing to pay any fines.

- 416 Eindeckers were built by Fokker in four variants, with the E.III being the most numerous.

- Although the Eindecker's fuselage and wings were usually fabric covered, Fokker had E.III E.365/16 covered with transparent Cellon in an effort to render the machine 'invisible' in the air. However, this smooth covering wrinkled badly when subjected to moisture, and at some angles the Cellon caused strong reflections that blinded the pilot and left the Eindecker highly visible!

- Although thoroughly obsolete by the autumn of 1916, the Eindecker remained the favourite of 18-victory ace Ltn Kurt Wintgens because the E.IV variant boasted two machine guns – double the firepower of its biplane successors like the Albatros D.I and Halberstadt D.III/V.

*Below:* **French Poilu pose proudly with a captured Eindecker that they have dismantled for transport to the rear lines for inspection.** *via Aviation-images.com*

## SPECIFICATIONS

### Fokker E.III

| | |
|---|---|
| **Engine:** | Oberursel U I |
| **Power:** | 100hp |
| **Max Speed:** | 87.5mph (140km/h) |
| **Length:** | 23ft 9.5in (7.25m) |
| **Wingspan:** | 32ft 11.6in (10.04 m) |
| **Height:** | 8ft 0.5in (2.45m) |
| **Armament:** | One 7.92mm LMG 08 machine gun |
| **Max all-up weight:** | 1,341lb (608kg) |
| **Range:** | endurance of 2.5 hours |
| **Number built:** | around 272 E.IIIs |
| **Entered service:** | late 1915 |

# IN COMBAT

EINDECKERS BEGAN arriving on the Western Front from the Fokker factory at Schwerin in the early summer of 1915. It initially took the Germans a little time to work out how best to operate this revolutionary new machine, aircraft being attached in ones and twos to Feldflieger Abteilungen. These units operated two-seat reconnaissance biplanes, and it was initially hoped that one Eindecker per unit would be sufficient to perform escort and local defence tasks. By the end of July 1915 there were 15 Eindeckers on the Western Front, and

during the course of that month the aircraft was credited with its first victories.

Future aces Ltn Oswald Boelcke and Ltn d R Max Immelmann soon began to make their presence felt over the frontlines, both pilots finding that poorly defended Allied reconnaissance aircraft were easy prey for the Fokker fighter. Tactics employed by the Eindecker units steadily improved, and as the number of fighters increased and their pilots gained further experience, the toll inflicted on Allied squadrons grew alarmingly. Indeed, by the end of 1915 the terms 'Fokker fodder' and 'Fokker scourge' were being mentioned in Allied reconnaissance units.

One such individual who encountered an Eindecker in combat during this period was future high-scoring ace James McCudden. *'To see a Fokker just steadying itself to shoot another machine in the air is, when seen close up, a most impressive sight, for there is no doubt that the Fokker in the air was an extremely unpleasant looking beast'*. Allied reconnaissance flights were so threatened that the RFC revised its tactics, issuing an order on 14 January 1916 that 'until the RFC is in

*Above:* **The pilot opens up his aeroplane's 100hp Oberursel rotary engine as he heads off for another mission over the front line in his Fokker E.III.**
*via Aviation-images.com*

*Right:* **The remains of Rittm Erich Graf von Holck's E.III after his encounter with escadrille N3 on 30 April 1916, in which the close friend of future 'Red Baron', Ltn Manfred Frhr von Richthofen, was killed by Lt Albert Deullin.**
*via Author*

## ACES

Oswald Boelcke scored the most victories in an Eindecker – 19 out of his final tally of 40. Eleven pilots scored five or more victories in the Eindecker. Boelcke, Immelmann and Wintgens all received Germany's highest military decoration, the Pour le Mérite or 'Blue Max', while flying the Eindecker, after each pilot passed the then-required eight victory total for each aviator.

High-scoring Eindecker ace Oblt Oswald Boelcke (left) gets a visit from Kronprinz Wilhelm of Prussia, commander of the 5 Armee. Boelcke's airfield at Sivry was not far from the crown prince's headquarters at Stenay, and the two men became good friends. *via Author*

possession of a machine as good as or better than the German Fokker, a machine proceeding on reconnaissance must be escorted by at least three other flying machines'.

In early 1916 the Germans began grouping single-seaters together for special operations, thus greatly increasing their effectiveness in the air. These Kampfeinsitzer Kommandos would eventually form the nuclei for permanent single-seat fighter units, known as Jagdstaffeln. By then there were more than 80 Eindeckers in the frontline.

*Above:* **An Eindecker pilot gamely waves at the photographer as he cruises at 80mph over German-held territory in Belgium in late 1915.** *via Aviation-images.com*

*Right:* **Ltn Walter Höhndorf reclines on 'standby alert' atop his Fokker E.IV 437/15, which he flew with a fair amount of success with Fokkerstaffel Falkenhausen and KEK Vaux.** *via Author*

As previously noted, Boelcke and Immelmann were the most successful pilots to fly the Fokker monoplane, the former claiming 19 victories and the latter 17 (or 15 depending on source) with the Eindecker. A further nine pilots claimed five or more aerial victories. However, gun stoppages and synchronisation problems, engine unreliability and the unwieldy nature of the Eindecker meant that the fighter was never a firm favourite with its pilots. By the spring of 1916 its invincibility was being challenged by a new breed of Allied fighters such as the DH2 pusher and the Nieuport 11, which were more manoeuvrable and technically superior to the Fokker monoplane. The German high command was slow to replace the Eindecker, which meant that the Allies quickly gained aerial superiority at the Battle of the Somme in July 1916. This had changed by year-end, however, with the fielding of the superb D-Type biplane fighters.

Elsewhere, Eindeckers also saw combat in small numbers in Palestine with the German-Turkish Expeditionary Force, over Gallipoli, on the Eastern Front and with the Austro-Hungarians on the Italian Front.

# SURVIVORS

ONLY ONE ORIGINAL Eindecker remains. On 8 April 1916, a novice German pilot took off from Valenciennes with a new E.III bound for Wasquehal, but became lost in haze and landed at a British aerodrome east of St Omer. The captured E.III was test-flown against the Morane-Saulnier N and other Allied types at St Omer before going to Upavon in Wiltshire for evaluation and finally going on museum display. It now resides at the Science Museum in London.

*Science Museum/Science & Society Picture Library*

# AIRCO DH2

**THE PUSHER SCOUTS** of the British and French air arms in 1916-17 were the first fighters to enter service with the Allies in World War One, and they took the fight to the German 'Fokker scourge'. These machines were named 'pushers' simply because their engine was mounted at the rear of the aircraft, rather than in the nose. In early 1916, No 24 Squadron, with its Aircraft Manufacturing Company (Airco) DH2s, became the first single-seat fighter unit in the Royal Flying Corps. Ungainly yet nimble, the DH2 helped the Allies attain air superiority over the Somme in the spring of 1916 and hold through that bloody summer. The DH2 was more than a match for the by-now obsolete Fokker Eindecker.

A superb DH2 replica flying in the colours of No 24 Squadron. Despite its fragile looks, the DH2 was an agile beast that helped put an end to the 'Fokker Scourge' in early 1916.
*Darren Harbar*

When aviation pioneer George Holt Thomas wanted to expand his business from manufacturing airships into aircraft design and construction, he was advised to contact a 26-year-old aircraft designer by the name of Geoffrey de Havilland. Born on 27 July 1882, de Havilland had helped design and develop such legendary aeroplanes as the BE and FE series, but by 1914 he wanted to design his own machine. After talking to Holt Thomas, he signed on as Airco's chief designer and test pilot.

Holt Thomas directed de Havilland to begin design work on a two-seater pusher biplane. With the engine and propeller behind the pilot, the new scout could dispense with the then oft-unreliable interrupter gear needed to enable a machine gun to fire through a propeller arc.

With experience from working on previous pusher designs, de Havilland set about creating the DH1. A two-seater powered by a 70hp Renault V8 engine, the aircraft was armed with a telescopically mounted Lewis machine gun that could be fired by the observer seated in the front cockpit.

The war with Germany that everybody had expected finally broke out that August, and work on the DH1 became a priority. The prototype was completed in February 1915, but by then the RFC favoured use of the RAF's FE2a, which carried a larger payload than the DH1.

Undeterred, de Havilland and his design team of Charles Walker and Howard Ker concentrated on a single-seat pusher biplane — born from a scaled down version of the DH1 — which became known as the DH2. The biplane design sandwiched a streamlined wood and metal nacelle that held the pilot, fuel tank and 100hp Gnome Monosoupape rotary engine, with twin booms leading back to the empennage. de Havilland made the inaugural flight in the aircraft on 1 June 1915 and reported that it was tail heavy, but after employing some weight-saving measures and moving the nacelle

forward four inches the craft flew satisfactorily two weeks later with a top speed of 88mph at 6,000ft. The chosen armament was a Lewis machine gun that was externally mounted to port within an aluminium fairing, and this could be elevated by the pilot.

On 22 June the prototype was evaluated by Capt Robert Maxwell Pike, who suggested installing streamlined flying wires to increase speed and angling the vertical stabiliser to starboard to counter engine torque. Overall, Pike thought the DH2's visibility was the best of any aeroplane he had ever flown, and that he *'has not seen a German machine which can equal this Scout for speed and climbing power'*. Following alterations, the prototype was assigned serial number 4732 and in late July it was sent to France for in-service evaluation with the RFC's No 5 Squadron. Unfortunately, on 9 August Pike was mortally wounded by a German two-seater observer, but before dying he crash-landed behind enemy lines, giving the Germans a mostly intact and up-close preview of their new adversary.

Regardless of the loss, Airco conducted further alterations to its design, the most notable of which was moving the Lewis gun from its external mount and relocating it within the cockpit atop a central mounting bracket. The first production batch was ordered in September 1915, and these machines began appearing that November. Subsequent 100-machine production batches were ordered in March and August 1916, followed by a 50-aircraft production order in October and a final 100 machines ordered in September 1916. Changes during these production orders included replacing the two-bladed propeller with one of four blades, relocating the gravity fuel tank from the upper wing's undersurface to its uppersurface, enlargement of the ailerons, employing a balanced rudder and various alterations with the layout of the cockpit instrumentation.

The business end of No 32 Squadron DH2 7851. The interchangeability of the wings is well evident in this view. Note the subtle aileron sag, fuselage ammunition bins outside the cockpit and the additional fairing surrounding the Lewis machine gun. *via Author*

*Left:* **The DH2 shows off the agility that allowed Lanoe Hawker (in whose colours this replica is finished), to become an ace.**
*Darren Harbar*

*Below left:* **No 32 Squadron's Capt Herman von Poellnitz beats up Vert Galand airfield in the summer of 1916. The aeroplane boasts interplane strut streamers and 'C' Flight markings on the wheel covers.**
*via Author*

THE FIRST DH2s arrived at the Central Flying School in December 1915 and four were sent to Nos 5, 11 and 18 Squadrons in France for evaluation in early 1916. The machine arrived on the Continent in earnest with No 24 Squadron in February 1916, and by late May Nos 29 and 32 Squadrons had also been equipped with the nimble machines. 1916 saw 222 DH2s serve with the British Expeditionary Force (BEF) in France. DH2s also saw combat with the Middle East Brigade.

Soon after entering service in the spring of 1916 the DH2 suffered a chronic engine failure 'pandemic'. Squadron record books and combat accounts are filled with reports of 'engine went dud', 'engine cutting out', 'engine going very badly', 'engine cut out on two cylinders and started to knock', 'engine ran well for first three-quarters of an hour then became rough and missed'.

Overall, the DH2 was an initial success. Born from necessity to overcome the challenge of firing a machine gun through a spinning propeller arc, the fighter was sullied by rumour and hamstrung by engine problems. Yet it was flown into battle by the RFC, where it faced down the 'Fokker Scourge'. 1916 was unquestionably the DH2's year, initially dominating the skies but subsequently enduring a hard fought fall from grace.

# KNIGHTS OF THE AIR

## John Oliver Andrews

The son of a brewer, John Oliver Andrews was born on 20 July 1896 in Waterloo, Lancashire. He graduated from Manchester High School in 1912, and two years later joined the Royal Scottish Regiment as a 2nd Lieutenant. Shortly thereafter Andrews was seconded to the RFC for training as an observer, and in that capacity he served with No 5 Squadron in 1915. Realising the war was going to be much longer than anticipated, Andrews trained to be a pilot and received his Royal Aeroclub certificate in October 1915, after which he joined No 24 Squadron then forming in England. With that unit he trained to fly DH2s.

In February 1916 No 24 Squadron travelled to France, and by that autumn Andrews had been credited with seven victories, including Jasta 2 Staffelführer and Oswald Boelcke successor Oblt Stefan Kirmaier. The following day he was involved in the legendary fight with Jasta 2 that saw No 24 Squadron's CO and RFC luminary Maj Lanoe Hawker shot down and killed by the rising Jasta 2 star, Manfred von Richthofen.

*via Author*

Afterwards, Andrews flew Sopwith Pups as a No 66 Squadron flight commander and later commanded the RAF's No 209 Squadron. Andrews eventually retired from the RAF with the rank of air vice-marshal in 1945 and died on 29 May 1989.

## Lanoe Hawker

Lanoe George Hawker was the first ace of the British Commonwealth. An aggressive combat pilot, his motto was 'Attack Everything!' Flying a BE2c armed with a few bombs and hand grenades, he successfully attacked the Zeppelin shed at Gontrode in April 1915 and was awarded the Distinguished Service Order. Hawker, with assistance from Air Mechanic Ernest Elton, devised a mount for attaching a Lewis gun to the Bristol Scout in June 1915. While testing his invention, he chased off one German aircraft and drove down two others. For this action, he was the first pilot to receive the Victoria Cross for aerial combat.

# FACT FILE

## CONSTRUCTION

### FUSELAGE

A stubby nacelle of cable-braced ash and spruce framework supported a plywood floor, aluminium top and nose, with sides of stitched fabric. The engine was bolted to the rear of the nacelle, with the fuel and oil tanks located immediately forward of it behind the pilot. In lieu of a fuselage, the DH2 had twin upper and lower wire-braced and spruce strut-supported tubular steel booms that bracketed the propeller and extended back to the empennage.

### COCKPIT

The pilot sat in a low-sided cockpit, restrained in his wicker seat by a wide lap belt. Instrumentation included an altimeter, airspeed indicator, tachometer, bubble inclinometer, air pressure valve and gauge, oil pulsator glasses and a floor-mounted compass. A conventional control column and rudder bar provided pilot control about the axes.

### TAIL

The empennage consisted of a steel tube framed and spruce ribbed horizontal stabiliser with a spruce framed vertical stabiliser above, all covered by doped fabric. The elevators and counter balanced rudder were similarly constructed and controlled by the pilot via cables that led to the cockpit.

### WINGS

Aerodynamic lift was provided by four subtly tip-tapered wings of equal span that had different chords on either side of the boom attachments. The wings were rigged without stagger or sweepback, but employed approximately four degrees of dihedral, and all were identical.

### ARMAMENT

The DH2 was armed with a single air-cooled Lewis Mk 1 machine gun that fired 0.303in ammunition at a rate of approximately 550 rounds per minute. Bullets were stored in circular 47- or 97-cartridge magazines (or 'drums') that required changing by the pilot in combat — replacement 'drums' were housed in external racks on either side of the cockpit.

### UNDERCARRIAGE

The main undercarriage featured cable-braced ash V-struts to which a rubber cord sprung axle supported spoked wheels. The empennage was supported by a spring-cushioned steel-shoed ash tailskid.

### ENGINE

The standard engine used by the DH2 was the 100hp Gnome Monosoupape 9 Type B-2, a normally aspirated, air-cooled, nine-cylinder rotary motor. Being an air-cooled rotary engine, the Gnome Monosoupape rotated with the propeller.

## SPECIFICATIONS

### DH2

| | |
|---|---|
| Engine: | Gnome Monosoupape |
| Power: | 100hp |
| Max Speed: | 93mph (150km/h) |
| Length: | 23ft 2in (7.68m) |
| Wingspan: | 28ft 3in (8.61m) |
| Height: | 9ft 6in (2.9m) |
| Armament: | One 0.303in Lewis Mk 1 machine gun |
| Max all-up weight: | 1,441lb (654kg) |
| Range: | 220 miles (354km) |
| Number built: | 400 |
| Entered service: | February 1916 |

**914**

**arch:**
eoffrey de
villand signs on
th the Aircraft
anufacturing
ompany (Airco)
chief aeroplane
signer and test
ot.

**1915**

**June:**
de Havilland
conducts inaugural
DH2 flight and
begins series of
test flights and
refinements.

**9 August:**
DH2 prototype
sent to France
for combat
evaluation is
shot down and
captured mostly
intact by the
Germans.

**1916**

**February:**
DH2 arrives in
France with
No 24 Squadron.

**I July:**
The Battle of the Somme
commences. British Army
suffers 60,000 killed or
wounded on the first day
of the offensive. DH2 units
soon wrest control of the
skies over the battlefield
from Eindeckers, thus ending
the 'Fokker Scourge'.

**23 November:**
No 24 Squadron
commanding officer and RFC
luminary Maj Lanoe Hawker
is shot down and killed
by Jasta 2's Manfred von
Richthofen after an eight-
minute swirling dogfight
and race to the lines near
Bapaume, France.

**1917**

**June:**
Nos 24 and 32
Squadrons are
the last frontline
units in France
to replace their
DH2s, receiving
DH5s in their
place.

Airco DH2, 7858, of Flt Sgt J. T. B. McCudden, No 29 Squadron.
James McCudden became an ace (five victories) in DH2s to start
his career as the British Empire's fourth ranking ace of the
war (total victories 57). *Courtesy Osprey Publishing*

Darren Harbar

# DID YOU KNOW?

● The pilot had to aim and fire the DH2's
single machine gun whilst flying the aircraft
with the other hand. On production aircraft the traverse was
eliminated and eventually most squadrons found ways of
fastening down the rear of the gun.

● The DH2's Gnome Monosoupape (single-valve) rotary engine
tended to blow off its cylinders whilst running.

● The arrival of the DH2 over the Western Front quickly ended the
RFC's period as 'Fokker fodder', as it was superior to the once
unrivalled Eindecker.

● No fewer than 400 DH2s were constructed by Airco, with
266 sent to France in 1916, 32 to the Middle East and 100
equipping training units in Britain. The remaining two flew with
Home Defence units.

● The DH2 was heavily committed during the Battle of the
Somme in July 1916, with No 24 Squadron alone fighting
no fewer than 774 combats and destroying 44
enemy machines.

Lt Geoffrey
H. Bonnell, an
American volunteer
in No 32 Squadon,
sits in the nacelle
of a DH2. Bonnell
would later join the
US Army Air Service
and command the 147th
Aero Squadron. *via Author*

# FROM THE COCKPIT

THE DH2 AROSE from the need for a fast single-seat aeroplane armed with a forward-firing machine gun at a time when the still unreliable synchronisation gear necessitated that such a machine be of pusher design.

Pilot engine management included a magneto switch, a fine adjustment wheel for fuel and an on/off 'blip switch' on top of the control column. There was no throttle – the Gnome Monosoupape was either off or running at full power – so the blip switch supplied a means of pilot engine control by 'blipping' or momentarily cutting off the magnetos that supplied current to the spark plugs. If there was no spark there was no combustion. The engine still rotated when blipped and fuel/air mixture was still drawn into the cylinders, so when the pilot released the blip switch after a short interval the spark returned and combustion began anew.

Being an air-cooled rotary engine, the Gnome Monosoupape rotated with the propeller, which on early production DH2s was fixed pitch, two-bladed and wooden. In April 1916 tests showed the efficiency of a four-bladed propeller, and by that June all DH2s in France were so equipped.

The DH2's firepower consisted of a single forward-firing Lewis 0.303in machine gun with a rate of fire of approximately 550 rounds per minute. The Lewis was fed ammunition via a top-mounted rotating drum that contained 47 rounds – later 'double drums' held 97, reducing

crank, to which the elevator control cables were connected. Due to the DH2's pusher configuration, its pilots received no warming benefits from residual engine heat.

With a short wingspan and rear-mounted rotary engine, the DH2 was highly manoeuvrable. Conversely, however, these same attributes also meant that the aircraft had a worrying propensity to fall into a spin. Little was known about how or even whether one could recover from a spin at the time, but No 24 Squadron CO, Maj Lanoe Hawker, understood the concept of centralising the controls.

After hearing his pilots speak of the DH2's spinning tendencies in February 1916, Hawker wordlessly left the squadron mess, took a plane up to 8,000ft, deliberately put it into a spin and then pulled out of it. He repeated the performance several times, from right and left handed turns, then landed and rejoined his men in the mess. *'It's all right, you fellows'*, he announced. *'You can get the DH2 out of any spin. I have just tried it out'*. His men promptly practiced at his technique and No 24 had no

> ## 'IT WAS A VERY HANDY AEROPLANE
> ## WHEN THE ENGINE WAS
> ## FUNCTIONING PROPERLY' 2Lt John Andrews

the frequency of cumbersome in-flight drum replacement to reload – which were externally housed in wooden bins that bracketed the cockpit. Double drums were stored internally due to their larger sizes. All of the above was housed within a stubby nacelle of cable-braced ash and spruce framework that supported a plywood floor, aluminium top and nose, with sides of stitched fabric. The pilot sat in a low-sided cockpit, restrained in his wicker seat by a wide lap belt. Instrumentation included an altimeter, airspeed indicator, tachometer, bubble inclinometer, air pressure valve and gauge, oil pulsator glasses and a floor-mounted compass. A conventional control column and rudder bar provided pilot control about the axes, and elevator trim was provided by a sprung-lever quadrant on the starboard bell

further spinning-related accidents. One of those pilots was future ace John Andrews, who recalled: *'The DH2 was quite a tricky little aeroplane, very different from the tractors (engine and propeller in front of the pilot) in which I'd done most of my flying. I had flown pusher types, such as the Farman and the Vickers, but the DH2 had a much smaller wingspan, was more heavily loaded and the torque of the comparatively large engine in a small frame was somewhat unusual in an aircraft of that period.*

*'One had to get accustomed to that very marked engine torque, which rocked the aeroplane, and tended to turn it instead of the airscrew. You had to be very careful to take no risks near the ground until you got a proper feel for the machine. There was a particular problem with spinning. Any aircraft which stalled easily and which was laterally unstable on account of the engine torque, tended to get into a spin. With the DH2, things happened very suddenly because of this torque, and unless you spotted it and corrected it at once, you could get into a spin or stall the engine.*

*'It was a very handy little aeroplane when the engine was functioning properly, and it had quite a lot of horses for the size of the aircraft, so it gave quite good performance.'*

## HAWKER v RICHTHOFEN

While flying a DH2, Lanoe Hawker left Bertangles Aerodrome on 23 November 1916 as part of 'A' Flight, led by Capt J. O. Andrews. Andrews led an attack on two German aircraft over Achiet, but spotting a larger flight of German aircraft above Andrews chose to break off the attack. Hawker, however, pressed on. Losing contact with the other DH2s, Hawker began a lengthy, circling dog-fight with the Albatros D.II flown by Manfred von Richthofen. Richthofen wrote of the dogfight in his autobiography: *'Thus we both turned like madmen in circles, with engines running full-throttle at 3,500m height. First 20 times left, then 30 times right, each mindful of getting above and behind the other.'*

As is the nature of a dogfight, the circling combatants began to lose altitude as each tried to gain the advantage over the other. The playing field was almost evenly matched as Hawker flew the DH2 capable of turning tighter circles and Richthofen piloted the Albatros D.II, which was faster. Hawker, however, had the dual disadvantage of being over German lines and a wind drift that would carry him even farther into enemy territory. Unable to get advantage over his opponent, Hawker broke away from the spiral and attempted a series of evasive aerobatics. Running out of both fuel and sky, Hawker finally had to make what was perhaps the only practical choice available to him – a low level dash back towards the Allied lines. Flying in a somewhat straight line only a few metres above the treetops, Richthofen, in the faster machine, now had the advantage. Hawker jinked his machine up and down and side-to-side in order to present a difficult target for Richthofen. 50 yards from the lines, however, a bullet from Richthofen's guns struck Hawker in the head, killing him instantly. His plane spun from 1,000ft and crashed. Lanoe Hawker went down in history as Richthofen's 11th victim.

*Painting by Russell Smith*

# IN COMBAT

THE FIRST UNIT to be equipped with production examples of the DH2 was No 24 Squadron, which arrived in France in February 1916. It initially shouldered the DH2's frontline workload alone, escorting two-seater reconnaissance aeroplanes as a result of dangers imposed by the EIII 'Fokker Scourge'. Inevitably, such missions brought the DH2 into conflict with the dreaded German machine, but soon the British pushers, and the men who flew them, began making names for themselves.

No 29 Squadron joined the fray with DH2s in mid April 1916, flying from Abeele, on the French/Belgian border. Yet things were relatively quiet for the unit initially since, according to future 32-victory ace 2Lt Geoffrey Hilton Bowman, 'we were in the Ypres Salient and all the Huns had gone down to the Somme'. Squadron mate and future 57-victory ace Flt Sgt James McCudden concurred that German machines were 'quite inactive' throughout the

summer. No 32 Squadron arrived in-theatre in early June, on 1 July (the first day of the Somme offensive) its CO, ace Capt Lionel Rees, earned himself the Victoria Cross for single-handedly attacking a formation of 10 German two-seaters, destroying two of them.

The Battle of the Somme was almost certainly the DH2's moment of glory as units equipped with the fighter wrested control of the sky from the previously dominant Eindeckers. However, this success was short-lived glory, for during the autumn of 1916 the Albatros D.II established the single-seat tractor-engined biplane as the most efficient killing machine in the sky. Nevertheless, RFC pilots serving with Nos 24, 29 and 32 Squadrons scored some remarkable successes during the early months of 1917, despite the obsolescence of the mount. Indeed, no fewer than 14 pilots claimed five or more victories with the DH2 in 1916-17, Irishman Lt Patrick Langan-Byrne of No 24 Squadron being the leading ace with 10. He was killed on 16 October 1916 by the legendary German ace Oswald Boelcke, Langan-Byrne being his 34th victim.

The aircraft remained in frontline service in France, however, until Nos 24 and 32 Squadrons completed their re-equipment in June 1917.

## ACES

Distinguished pilots of the DH2 included Victoria Cross winner Lanoe Hawker (seven victories), Alan Wilkinson (10) and Patrick Langan-Byrne (also 10). Lionel Rees won the Victoria Cross flying the DH2 for single handedly attacking a formation of 10 German two-seaters on 1 July 1916, destroying two. James McCudden became an ace in DH2s to start his career as the British Empire's fourth ranking ace of the war. Fourteen aces scored five or more aerial victories using the DH2; many went on to further success in later types also.

## SURVIVORS

IT'S NOT KNOWN when the last DH2 was scrapped, however there were clearly none left by the time preservation in early aircraft began to emerge. It was not until many years later that renewed interest in the type manifested itself in the form of construction of a full-scale flying replica. The late Walt Redfern produced a fine reproduction DH2 and made the drawings available to homebuilders.

# NIEUPORT 17

**THE NIEUPORT 17C-1** – meaning Type 17 chasse (fighter), one seat – was one of the greatest Allied combat aircraft of World War One. Although the belated availability of synchronised guns in Allied fighters did much to redress the balance during the latter half of 1916, the 'Fokker Scourge' was finally ended by the delivery of machines such as the Nieuport 17. Many hundreds of Nieuport 17s served with the RFC, the RNAS, the French Aéronautique Militaire, Russia, Holland, Italy, Belgium, Finland and the USA. The Nieuport 17 was the fighter of choice for the famous Escadrille des Cicognes and Escadrille Lafayette and of aces such as Bishop, Ball, Guynemer and Nungesser. The follow-on Nieuport 23 and 27 were similar to the 17 but with a rounded tail.

**The aircraft of aces, the nimble Nieuport 17 helped turn the tide of aerial combat during World War One.**
*via AirTeamImages.com*

At the start of World War One, the battlefield commanders did not view the role of the 'new-fangled' flying machine seriously. However, as the conflict progressed, the value of aerial reconnaissance soon became apparent. This in turn spurred on the development of aircraft to stop the enemy from seeing what was happening on their side of the lines. Thus aerial combat began. Within two years of the fighter's debut as a distinctive aircraft type over the Western Front, a number of possible configurations had been examined. These included triplanes, quadruplanes and even quintuplanes. Most were quickly discarded, with the biplane and the monoplane emerging predominant. There was one promising alternative, however, and this was the sesquiplane – a biplane in which the lower wing possessed less than half the area of the upper. The leading exponent of this compromise configuration was Gustave Delage, chief engineer of Nieuport.

Founded by Edouard de Niéport in 1906, the Societé Anonyme des Établissments Nieuport had already acquired a healthy reputation among aircraft builders with a series of simple, robust monoplanes, but its fortunes were to be revolutionised when Delage joined in January 1914. His first design, the Type X, began as a two-seat monoplane to compete in the Gordon-Bennett Trophy race. When war erupted, however, the French Army declared a preference for a reconnaissance biplane, which in turn led Delage to alter his design into a compromise that he hoped would combine the best traits of biplane and monoplane.

Although designated Type XB – the 'B' referred to its biplane configuration – Delage's modified aeroplane employed a wing cellule consisting of a narrow chord, single spar lower wing that was essentially an almost horizontal bracing strut with an airfoil section for the more conventional two-spar upper wing. The wings had a slight sweepback of 2.75 degrees, this aerodynamic feature pervading subsequent designs up to the Nieuport 28. Another trait soon to be synonymous with Nieuport products was the lack of dihedral to the upper wing, while the lower wing's dihedral could be adjusted to as much as six degrees. Delage's 'one-and-a-half wing' design came to be referred to as a sesquiplane, the shape of its interplane struts also earning his creations the English sobriquet of 'vee-strutters'.

The first single-seat fighter adhering to sesquiplane configuration was the 80hp Le Rhône-engined Nieuport 11 of 1915. Its lower wing was little more than a faired spar, providing girder bracing to the upper mainplane but extended outboard beyond the V-strut

## KNIGHTS OF THE AIR

### Charles Nungesser

Charles Eugene Marie Nungesser was born in Paris on 15 March 1882. Dropping out of school, he travelled to Brazil to work in his uncle's sugar plantation, but ended up finding employment in Argentina as a car mechanic. Nungesser then started racing cars professionally in South America at the age of 17, where he met a fellow Frenchman who had access to an aeroplane. He talked his friend into letting him take the Bleriot into the air by himself, and after flying it around for a few minutes he made a successful landing. Within two weeks Nungesser had refined his flying abilities and started his career in aviation.

Returning to France following the outbreak of war, he joined the 2nd Hussars as a private. Nungesser subsequently transferred to the Aéronautique Militaire and received his brevet on 2 March 1915. Initially serving with VB106, he then moved to N65 shortly after achieving his first victory flying a Voisin two-seater. Gaining his second success in December, Nungesser broke both of his legs in a crash on 6 February 1916 and remained out of the cockpit until the spring of that year. Now flying Nieuport Scouts, he had claimed 21 victories by the end of the year, despite having been wounded in action and injured yet again in a flying accident.

Despite being in and out of hospital for treatment to his previous injuries throughout 1917, Nungesser managed to persuade his superiors not to ground him. Attached to V116 with his own Nieuport 17, he had added nine victories to his tally by August 1917. In early 1918, Nungesser was assigned to SPA65 (his old unit, now re-designated), and although the rest of the escadrille flew SPADs, he stuck with Nieuport sesquiplanes. By war's end his tally stood at 43 victories and 11 probables, virtually all of which were claimed in Nieuport Scouts.

Post-war, Nungesser became transfixed with making a transatlantic flight from France to the USA. On 8 May 1927 Nungesser and his friend Francois Coli departed Le Bourget airport, near Paris, in a Levasseur PL8. Sadly they disappeared somewhere over the North Atlantic Ocean.

**Highly-decorated Charles Nungesser is seen here wearing both French and foreign medals, including the British Military Cross. Despite many flying accidents, he survived the war with 43 victories and 11 probables to his name, virtually all of his successes having been claimed in Nieuport Scouts.** *via Author*

attachment points to provide additional lifting surface. The Type 11 quickly acquired the affectionate sobriquet of Bébé.

During the course of 1916 some French ecadrille de chasse began installing 110hp rotary engines in their Nieuport 11s and Nieuport itself soon followed suit, designating the machine the Type 16. The more powerful engine made for a 5mph increase in speed and a considerable improvement in rate-of-climb. Pilots soon became aware of the price that came with that higher performance, however. The heavier, more powerful, Le Rhône 9Ja made the Nieuport 16 nose heavy and manoeuvrability was more sluggish than with the Type 11. Although the Type 16s saw a good amount of French use, it took an outstanding pilot to master its idiosyncrasies. The obvious solution to the Type 16's intrinsic handling problems was to restore its centre of gravity and overall balance with an increased wing area, and that it precisely what the manufacturer did with its Type 17...

## THE NIEUPORT 17

was an immediate success. Apart from its increased wing area, 110hp Le Rhône engine and refinements to the basic airframe, it also incorporated Alkan-Hamy interrupter gear allowing the installation of a 0.303in Vickers machine gun on the fuselage upper decking. The Nieuport 17 entered combat in May 1916, and quickly replaced the Types 11 and 16 alike in frontline service. It was responsible, along with the DH2 for defeating the Fokker monoplanes with their synchronised

guns. Many famous French pursuit squadrons were early converts to the Nieuport 17, and RFC units started to receive them from mid-July 1916 too – these came via the RNAS. By the autumn the RFC had ordered many more. The fighter proved to be an outstanding success despite a propensity towards wing shedding. It equipped every French ecadrille de chasse at some point in 1916, the Type 17 establishing new standards of efficiency in its class to become the dominant French fighter until its own eventual eclipse by the SPAD VII.

By late July 1917, however, the Nieuport vee-strutters were looking, and performing, like tired veterans... the day of the Nieuport 17 over the Western Front was past. However, rather than design an entirely new replacement, Delage obsessively persisted with the refinement of what was by now a thoroughly outmoded basic design. He duly produced the Type 17bis with a 130hp Clerget 9B engine and fully faired fuselage sides, the Type 23, which was scarcely distinguishable from the Type 17, and the Type 24. None could match the contemporary SPAD VII and XIII for speed, durability or firepower. Nevertheless, they soldiered on in other roles to the end of the war thanks to the soundness and logic of their simple design. Total production of all Le Rhône-engined Nieuports reached approximately 7,200 aircraft.

Sgte Guido Nardini, or 'Rigoletto' as his friends called him, stands in front of a Nieuport 17 whose serial is unknown. The photograph was autographed by the pilot on 30 June 1917, 16 days after he scored his first victory, over a Brandenburg, which crashed in flames on the slopes of Monte Arhentera. *via Author*

*Above:* **Nieuport 23 N3598 flown by No 19 (Death or Glory) Squadron, the Russian Imperial Army Air Service. In November 1917 the aeroplane was captured by Austro-Hungarian troops.** *via Author*

*Left:* **An impressive line of Nieuports ready for inspection at Issouden, France. Nearest the camera is Nieuport 17, 2587.**

# CONSTRUCTION

### FUSELAGE

Like the Nieuport 11/16 before it, the Type 17 had a box section fuselage aft of the cockpit. The forward fuselage, however, was fully faired in aluminium to meet the circular engine cowling made of the same material. The wooden box fuselage had a rounded top decking, with pronounced upward sweep behind the engine and modest vertical taper toward the tail. .

### COCKPIT

The pilot sat in a plywood-backed seat that featured a leather-covered cushion. His cockpit was equipped with rudimentary instruments, including a clock, tachometer, airspeed indicator, altimeter, and oil pressure gauge, fuel gauge and compass. The trigger for the fuselage mounted Vickers machine gun was affixed to the control column. There was a rudimentary gunsight positioned just forward of the windscreen.

### WINGS

Undoubtedly the Nieuport scout's most distinctive feature, the sesquiplane (one-and-a-half) wing configuration was very much in evidence with the Type 17. The flying surfaces retained the standard wood and fabric construction of earlier Nieuports but differed from previous models in that the top wing had two spars. The Type 17 also had unequal chord ailerons and its vee-shaped interplane struts were bound with tape and wire braced. Four vertical struts held the top wing above the forward fuselage. The lower wing had slight dihedral, giving the sesquiplane its characteristic look in the air. The top wing was exactly twice the area of the bottom wing.

### ARMAMENT

Nieuport 17s flown by units of the Aéronautique Militaire were fitted with French-designed Alkan-Hamy interrupter gear that permitted the installation of a 0.303in Vickers machine gun on the fuselage upper decking in front of the cockpit. RFC and RNAS machines were generally armed with a Lewis 0.303in gun fitted to a rail-based Foster overwing mount devised by No 11 Squadron. The Lewis gun was fed ammunition from a 47-round removable drum. Some French Type 17s had both the synchronised Vickers gun and a Lewis gun on the upper wing attached to a Moreau mount.

### UNDERCARRIAGE

Conventional vee-shaped undercarriage struts and a leaf-type spring tailskid were attached to the aircraft's lower fuselage.

### ENGINE

The basic Type 17 was fitted with a 110hp nine-cylinder air-cooled Le Rhône 9Ja rotary engine, which replaced the company's 80hp 9C. Subsequently, the Type 17bis was fitted with the 130hp Clerget 9B engine and the Type 21 with an 80hp or 120hp Le Rhône – the latter motor also powered the Type 27.

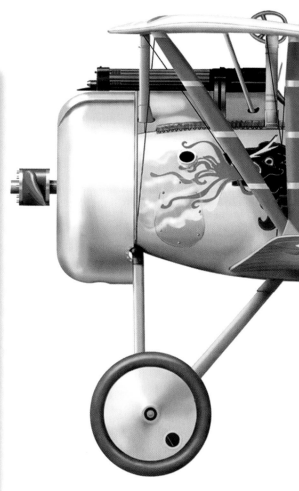

**Flamboyantly-decorated Nieuport 17 flown by Lt Maurice Boyeau, of Escadrille N77, summer of 1917.**
*Courtesy Osprey Publishing*

## SPECIFICATIONS

### Nieuport 17

| | |
|---|---|
| Engine: | Le Rhône 9Ja |
| Power: | 113hp |
| Max Speed: | 103mph (165 km/h) |
| Length: | 19ft (5.80 m) |
| Wingspan: | 26ft 9in (8.16m) |
| Height: | 7ft 10in (2.40m) |
| Armament: | One 0.303in Vickers synchronised machine gun and one 0.303in Lewis Mk1 on an overwing mount |
| Max all-up weight: | 1,232lb (560kg) |
| Range: | 186 miles (300km) |

### 1916

**January:**
The prototype Nieuport 17 makes its first flight.

**March:**
Early production examples reach the Aéronautique Militaire.

**4 May:**
Escadrille N57 gives the Type 17 its combat debut over the Western Front.

POIDS UTILE
120ᵏ

## DID YOU KNOW?

- The Nieuport sesquiplane family of fighters was so revered by the Germans on the Western Front that a handful of captured examples were repainted with crosses and used by future aces. One such individual was Uffz Paul Baümer, who made several 'front flights' in a Nieuport 23, formerly of No 60 Squadron RFC, which had been brought down unscathed on 6 May 1917.

- Most French aces used the nimble Nieuport 17 during their career including Georges Guynemer, Charles Nungesser, Maurice Boyau, Armand Pinsard, Réné Dorne, Gabriel Guerin, Alfred Duellin and Jean Navarre.

- Many early Nieuport 17s featured a so-called cône de penetration, a hemispherical fixed fairing mounted on an extension of the stationary crankshaft.

- Although not a single example of an original Nieuport 17 survives, Type 23 N5024 is on display in the outstanding Musée Royal de l'Armée in Brussels. Obtained by the Royal Army Museum in the 1920s, the aircraft was comprehensively restored in the early 2000s and then put back on display in November 2006.

*via AirTeamImages.com*

*Left:* **This Nieuport 17 was flown by Italian 20-victory ace Fulco Ruffo di Calabria between December 1916 and April 1917. Once in combat Ruffo quickly learned that a fundamental rule of air combat was to open fire at point blank range. On 28 February 1917, for example, he was so close to the enemy's tail when he fired that the Austrian crew reported that they had been able to see the black skull insignia on the Nieuport that had 'rammed' them.**
*via Author*

### 1917

**July:**
The RFC receives its first Type 17s, these aircraft having originally been ordered by the RNAS.

**16 August:**
Capt Albert Ball of No 60 Squadron claims the first of 23 victories in the Nieuport 17.

**January:**
The Italian Air Service issues French-built Nieuport 17s to frontline units.

**February:**
Trials commence of the Nieuport 24, which was essentially a Type 17 fitted with a new aerofoil section, wooden tail unit and 130hp engine.

**March:**
First of at least 80 Nieuport 23s enter service with the RFC.

**June:**
RFC starts to replace its Type 17s with Sopwith Camels.

**September:**
The American Expeditionary Force acquires 75 Nieuport 17s for training.

# FROM THE COCKPIT

CANADIAN ACE 'Billy' Bishop claimed no fewer than 36 of his 72 official victories in the Nieuport 17, despite only flying the type for four months with No 60 Squadron in 1917. He wrote at some length about the French scout following his posting to le Hameau aerodrome.

**No 1 Squadron's Capt W. W. Rogers in his Nieuport.** *via Author*

Joining the unit on 9 March 1917, Bishop noted in his diary: *'The first day of my stay with the squadron there was no flying, and so I wandered about the field hangars looking at the machines. They were all of a type I had never seen before at close range – Nieuport Scouts, very small and, of course, with but a single seat. Being a French model, the Nieuport Scout is a beautiful creature. The distinctly British machines are strictly built for business, with no particular attention paid to the beauty of the lines. The French, however, never overlook such things.*

*'We newcomers at the squadron had to stand by the next day and watch the patrols leaving to do their work over the lines. It was thrilling even to us, accustomed as we were to ordinary flying, to see the trim little fighters take to the air, one after the other, circle about the aerodrome, and then, dropping into a fixed formation, set their courses to the east. That night we listened with eager ears to the discussion of a fight in which a whole patrol had been engaged. We stay-at-homes had spent*

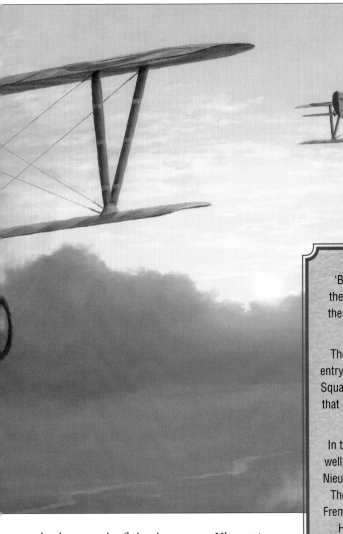

## LAFAYETTE ESCADRILLE

'By the Dawn's Early Light' is a tribute to the men and machines of the famed Lafayette Escadrille. Here we see three famous pilots from the escadrille – Lufbery, Thaw and Hill – on a morning patrol over the Western Front sometime during autumn of 1916.

The Lafayette Escadrille was formed in April of 1916, prior to the US entry into World War One. It had the unique distinction of being a French Squadron made up almost entirely of American Volunteers. The machine that is perhaps most associated with the Escadrille was the Nieuport 17, as depicted.

In the foreground we see Raoul Lufbery, the highest scoring and most well-known pilot of the Lafayette Escadrille. Lufbery is at the controls of Nieuport 17 N1844, a machine assigned to the group's Captain, Georges Thennault, but usually associated with Lufbery. A quiet man of mixed French and American descent, Lufbery took great care of his equipment. His plane was always the best in the squadron, as noted by fellow pilot Edward Hinkle, *'Anyone would rather have a secondhand Lufbery machine than a new one anytime'.* In the lead, flying N1803, is Lt William Thaw. Thaw was one of the original founders of the Lafayette Escadrille and is credited with the idea of using the famous Seminole Indian head as the group's logo. Finally, below and beyond Lufbery is Dudley Hill, flying N1950. Hill was blind in one eye but passed his medical by memorising the eye chart. He was a well-liked pilot and managed to log more flying time than any other escadrille member. *Painting by Russell Smith*

the day practise flying in our new Nieuports. There were three more days of this for me, and then, having passed some standard tests to show my familiarity with the Nieuport type, I was told to cross the lines for the first time as the master of my own machine.'

Bishop went out on his first patrol with No 60 Squadron on 17 Match 1917, flying Type 17 A274. The aircraft took off at 10.10hrs, the Canadian pilot subsequently noting the early moments of the flight in his diary.

'There is a click of the electric ignition switch, the propeller is given a sharp swing over, and the engine starts with a roar. Once or twice there is a cough, but pretty soon she is 'hitting' just right on every one of her multiple cylinders. It is all the mechanics can do to hold her back. Then the pilot throttles down to a very quiet little purr and signals to the attendants to draw away the chocks from under the wheels. Slowly you move forward under your own 'steam' and 'taxi' across the field rather bumpily, to head her into the wind. This accomplished, the throttle is opened wide, you rush forward with increasing speed, you feel the tail of the machine leave the ground, and then you go leaping into space.'

Although Bishop would quickly enjoy unparalleled success with the Type 17, the aircraft was still prone to the structural failures that had blighted previous Nieuport sesquiplanes. For example, on 7 June 1917 No 60 Squadron lost 2Lt Roland Harris whilst he was undertaking air-to-ground firing practice. Both starboard wings on his Nieuport collapsed, sending his aircraft into a vertical dive. Squadron commander Maj A. J. L. Scott immediately had himself helped into the cockpit of his Nieuport, whereupon he took off and continued the firing practice in an effort to restore confidence in the little biplane. An effort was made to prevent this wing failure by attaching an additional flying wire to the upper wing. It was generally believed that the primary cause of the failure was the use of unseasoned Canadian spruce in the spars and ribs.

# IN COMBAT

On 6 June 1917 Kapitan Evgraf Kruten, commander of the 2nd BAG, was returning from a flight when his Nieuport 17 N2232 suddenly went into a spin from a height of just 20-30m (65-100ft) and crashed on Plotychy airfield, killing the five-victory Russian ace. *via Author*

THE NIEUPORT 17 proved to be an outstanding success in frontline service, equipping every French escadrille de chasse at some point in 1916-17. The first examples of the improved sesquiplane had started to reach the Aéronautique Militaire in March 1916, the fighter initially being used alongside the Nieuport 11 and 16. The first unit to see action in the frontline with the Type 17 was Escadrille N57, which commenced patrols on 4 May.

Having flown both the Type 11 and 16, the Royal Flying Corps and the Royal Naval Air Service were also early customers for the Type 17. Early machines were issued to the RFC from July 1916, these aircraft having come via the RNAS, which had ordered them first. However, RFC reconnaissance aircraft desperately needed improved fighter protection during the Battle of the Somme, which was launched that same month. By the end of 1916 some 40 examples had been delivered to the RFC, with many more on order. Early users of the Nieuport Scout were Nos 1 and 60 Squadrons, followed by Nos 29 and 40 Squadrons – all four units were fully equipped with the Type 17 by the spring of 1917, as was 6 Naval Squadron.

The Type 17 and follow-on Type 23 also proved popular with other Allied air arms. In the west, the Belgian Air Service used the fighter to defend the north frontline that ended on the North Sea coast. All of the nation's leading aces flew the Nieuport at some stage in their careers as the fighter equipped all of Belgium's fighter escadrille in 1917, before being replaced by SPAD VIIs and Hanriots.

The US-manned Escadrille Lafayette, which was part of the Aéronautique Militaire from 1916, also received Nieuport 17s on the Western Front. Learning the art of aerial combat in the sesquiplane, many of these volunteer pilots subsequently joined the US Air Service in 1918 following America's belated entry into World War 1. Upon the American Expeditionary Force's arrival in France, it purchased 75 Nieuport 17s for training.

Further afield, the Italian Air Service used a substantial number of licence-built Nieuport Scouts over north and north-eastern Italy against the forces of the Austro-Hungarians. Initially, a handful of French-built machines were acquired, before production of 150 examples was commenced locally by Nieuport-Macchi. Once again, several of Italy's future aces flew Type 17s and 27s in 1917-18, before progressing to more advanced SPAD VIIs and XIIIs.

Finally, in the east the Russian Imperial Air Service started to introduce Type 17s into service from late 1916 to supplant Type 11s already in the frontline. By the end of that year there were 12 Fighter Detachments engaged in combat with the Germans over the Eastern Front, and while they flew a variety of equipment, the Nieuport Scouts were well to the fore prior to the eventual arrival of SPAD VIIs. Even then, Type 17s, 21s and 23s continued to see action until the time of the Revolution at the end of 1917.

## ACES

Aces of the calibre of Capts T. F. Hazell, Albert Ball and 'Billy' Bishop soon proved the worthiness of the Type 17, claiming high scores in 1916-17. Their French counterparts, men such as Georges Guynemer, Charles Nungesser and Maurice Boyau, enjoyed similar success as the sesquiplanes took on the new generation of Albatros scouts over the Western Front.

Nieuport 17s and 23s of the Russian Imperial Army Air Service's 3rd Battle Aviation Group (BAG) are prepared for their next mission at Dubno airfield, on the Western Front, during the summer of 1917. *via Author*

# BRISTOL F2 FIGHTER

**BUILT TO REPLACE** the obsolete two-seat types that had literally become 'Fokker fodder' over the Western Front, Bristol's F2A Fighter endured a disastrous combat debut in April 1917 when it suffered heavy losses at the hands of German single-seat Albatros scouts. However, crews quickly turned the tables when they realised that the replacement F2B had the speed and manoeuvrability only previously found in single-seat fighters. Pilots flew aggressively as if in a Camel or SE5A, aiming their fixed weapons, while their observers took shots at fighters that latched onto the tail of the F2B. Using these new tactics, the aircraft proved so effective that it began to produce aces with scores that rivalled those accrued by pilots of single-seat fighter types.

The muscular Bristol Fighter soon won the admiration of its crews and the respect of its adversaries.
*Darren Harbar*

'A curious feature of the types of British Aircraft of 1914-1918 was their marked individuality, like so many of those who flew them', wrote Maj W J F Harvey, 26-victory ace of World War 1. *'Some were hated, some, like the pretty kittenish Sopwith Pup, were loved, some, like the SE5 and the old workhorse FE2b, were respected for their sterling qualities. The*

## 'A FIGHTER BY NAME, INCLINATION AND APTITUDE' Maj Oliver Stewart, No 22 Squadron

*Farmans were funny jokes, one or two others were jokes in rather poor taste, and there was the Camel, that fantastic brainchild of Sopwith, which was both feared and respected. There was only one which was both respected and loved by all who flew it – the Bristol Fighter'.*

The Bristol Fighter's genesis began in 1916, when the Royal Flying Corps (RFC) began seeking a reconnaissance aeroplane to replace the all-too-stable and painfully vulnerable BE2c. The Royal Aircraft Factory, which created the BE, responded with the RE8, whose principal improvement was to exchange the pilot's and observer's positions, giving the latter a vastly improved field of fire.

Meanwhile, at British Aeroplane Ltd in Bristol, its chief engineer, Frank Sowter Barnwell, also offered a replacement in the form of the R2A, which featured a fuselage raised above the lower wing by struts in order to improve the pilot's view over the upper wing. A revised version of the Bristol design with unequal-span wings and a 150hp V8 Hispano-Suiza engine was designated the R2B, but it was quickly superceded by another variant with equal-span wings and a new 190hp Rolls-Royce Falcon I V12 engine. At that point, Barnwell's brainchild was being regarded as a 'reconnaissance-fighter'.

First flown in prototype form at Filton on 9 September 1916, the F2A soon had its vertical radiators replaced when it was found that they obscured the pilot's field of view during landing. A single annular radiator was fitted instead within the engine cowling. A3303 underwent its official tests between 16 and 18 October, using both a two and four-bladed propeller. The RFC was already impressed with the new aeroplane's potential, and testing only confirmed its decision to order 50 production examples.

One of the characteristic features of the F2 family that would become familiar for many years was the continuous lower wing structure, which was located 10 inches below the fuselage. The latter was 'carried' by struts attached to the lower fuselage longerons.

The second prototype, powered by a 150hp Hispano-Suiza, was flown on 25 October. This version was intended for production, but all Hispano-Suizas had by now been allocated to the SE5. The 50 F2As were to be powered by Rolls-Royce Falcon Is instead. Production aircraft would also feature blunt wingtips, which was a characteristic that remained unchanged throughout the production life of the Bristol Fighter.

Combining the agility of a single-seater, with the heavy fire power of a two-seater, the Bristol Fighter was a foe to be reckoned with. *Darren Harbar*

## FIGHTER OR SCOUT?

During World War One, the term 'fighter' was used more often for two-seat than single-seat aircraft. The latter were originally short-range reconnaissance aeroplanes appropriately called 'scouts'. Even after they were successfully armed with machine guns, the RFC continued to refer to single-seaters as scouts. Other nations, however, referred to them by terms reflecting their lone hunter status, such as the French 'avion de chasse', the German 'Jagdflugzeug' and American 'pursuit plane'. A fighter, on the other hand, was often thought of as a reconnaissance aeroplane with either the armament or performance to take care of itself.

## THE FIRST OPERATIONAL F2As

were delivered to No 48 Squadron in December 1916, armed with a synchronised 0.303in Vickers gun forward and a Lewis gun flexibly mounted on a Scarff ring in the observer's pit. After training at Rendcombe, in Gloucestershire, the unit was deployed to La Bellevue, in France, in March 1917, its aeroplanes being held until the start of the Battle of Arras in the hope of their achieving a degree of surprise over the enemy. Perhaps not coincidentally, the first of the Royal Aircraft Factory's latest 'Scout Experimentals' (better known as the SE5) was also to make its combat debut at that time, with No 56 Squadron.

The Bristol Fighter had a disastrous combat debut (see later) due to the implementation of poor tactics during what became known within the RFC as 'Bloody April'. Nevertheless, a further 200 machines were ordered for the RFC.

These aircraft would feature modified longer-span tailplanes and a slope to the upper fuselage longerons that improved the pilot's forward and downward visibility. The first 150 F2Bs, as the altered Bristols were officially designated, used Hispano-Suiza engines, but the next 50 were powered by the 220hp Rolls-Royce Falcon II, with radiator shutters to help control the engine's temperature.

At the end of May 1917, No 11 Squadron began replacing its FE2bs with F2As to become the second operational Bristol Fighter unit, although it only had five aircraft when it joined No 48 Squadron at La Bellevue on 1 June. By then, too, the first F2Bs had arrived to replace No 48 Squadron's depleted ranks.

# FACT FILE

## CONSTRUCTION

### FUSELAGE

The fuselage's square section box girder structure tapered to a horizontal knife edge aft, and the rear section was given more pronounced taper in side elevation. Forward of the cockpit, the Rolls-Royce Falcon was carried by steel tube engine bearers, with the annular radiator in front of the motor and a fuel tank immediately aft. A metal cowling covered the front of the fuselage as far back as the front top and bottom centre section wing struts, and the top of the fuselage back to the pilot's seat.

### COCKPIT

The pilot's cockpit was located under a large trailing edge cut-out and was pretty basic with standard layout of instruments to the front and throttle and mixture control to the left. Sat immediately behind the pilot, on a sliding seat, was the observer/gunner, his position fitted with a Scarff ring onto which was mounted a Lewis gun. Replacement ammunition drums for the weapon were stored within the rear cockpit.

### WINGS

A two-bay biplane, the F2 had wings of equal span. One of the aircraft's characteristic features was the continuous lower wing structure, which was located 10 inches below the fuselage. The latter was 'carried' by struts attached to the lower fuselage longerons. The centre section of the lower wing was an open structure on the F2A, with steel carry-through spars without fabric covering – it was covered over with the introduction of the F2B, however.

### ARMAMENT

The F2 was fitted with a centrally mounted, synchronised, forward-firing Vickers 0.303in machine gun that fired through a tube immediately above the engine and a Scarff ring-mounted Lewis weapon of a similar calibre for the observer. It could also carry up to 240lb of either 20lb Cooper or 112lb Hale bombs on underwing racks.

### UNDERCARRIAGE

A v-strutted main undercarriage assembly, fitted with elastic cord shock absorbers, was fitted with two large spoked wheels. The aircraft also featured a steerable sprung tailskid.

### ENGINE

The vast majority of F2s were powered by the hugely-successful Rolls-Royce Falcon V12 liquid-cooled engine. The F2A and first 150 F2Bs were fitted with Falcon Is, which produced 190hp. Fifty F2Bs had the Falcon II of 220hp installed, while most Fighters were equipped with the definitive Falcon III of 275hp. When supplies of the Falcon III failed to match production of F2 fuselages, the 200hp Sunbeam Arab was selected, but its performance was inferior.

## 1916

**28 August:**
Bristol receives an order for 50 F2A aircraft.

**9 September**
The first of two F2A prototypes makes its maide flight from Filto

## DID YOU KNOW?

- The United States Army Engineering Division planned to develop and build an American version of the Bristol Fighter. However, efforts to start production in the US stalled due to the decision to fit the 400hp Liberty L-12 engine which proved to be far too heavy and bulky making the Bristol nose heavy. Only 27 of the planned 2,000 were built.

- Only 52 F2As were produced before production switched to what became the definitive Bristol Fighter, the Type 14 F2B, which had first flown on 25 October 1916.
  In September and October 1917, orders for 1,600 F2Bs were placed, and by the end of World War 1 the RAF had 1,583 F2Bs in service.
  A total of 5,329 Bristol Fighters were eventually built, mostly by Bristol but also by companies such as Standard Motors and Armstrong Whitworth.

- Post-war, the F2B was used primarily in the Army Co-operation and dual-control training roles. Its durability ensured its survival in Iraq and the North-West Frontier of India until 1931.

## SPECIFICATIONS

### Bristol F2B Fighter

| | |
|---|---|
| Engine: | Rolls-Royce Falcon III |
| Power: | 275hp |
| Max Speed: | 125mph (201km/h) |
| Length: | 25ft 10in (7.87m) |
| Wingspan: | 39ft 3in (11.96m) |
| Height: | 9ft 9in (2.97m) |
| Armament: | One fixed Vickers 0.303in machine gun forward and one Lewis 0.303in for the observer. Underwing racks for 12 20lb bombs |
| Max all-up weight: | 2,800lb (1,280kg) |
| Range: | Three hour endurance |

**1917**

**cember:**

48 Squadron
omes the
t unit to
eive the F2A.

**8 March:**

No 48 Squadron
moves to
La Bellevue, in
France, on
8 March 1917.

**5 April:**

In what would become known
as Bristol's 'black day', No 48
Squadron gives the Fighter its
combat debut and loses four of
six aircraft to Albatros scouts.

**May:**

No 48 Squadron
receives the first
F2Bs to reach
the frontline.

**30 November:**

Ranking F2
ace Andrew
McKeever claims
his final victories,
taking his overall
tally to 31.

**1918**

**July:**

19 frontline
RAF units are
equipped with
the F2B.

**11 November:**

1,583 Bristol
Fighters are in
service with
the RAF on
Armistice Day.

**1919**

**September:**

Bristol delivers
the final F2Bs to
the RAF.

*Above:* **Bristol F2B
Fighter, C-4810, of
No 22 Squadron, RFC.
It was in this aircraft
that ace pilot Lt George
Bulmer and his gunner
2 Lt Percy Williams shot
down two Pfalz DIIIs in
one engagement on
16 March 1918.**
*Courtesy Osprey Publishing*

Darren Harbar

Darren Harbar

**IN CLOSE-UP**

SCHEDULE
FOR
ROLLS-ROYCE
FALCON
AERO-ENGINE

SERIES I AND II
WITH
ADDENDA
SERIES III

Darren Harbar

# FROM THE COCKPIT

A HANDFUL OF F2BS have been restored to airworthiness over the years. One of these machines, D7889, was flown on a number of occasions by well-known warbird pilot Stuart Goldspink. His impressions of the Fighter are as follows:

*'The first challenge facing the would-be Bristol Fighter pilot is just getting into the cockpit of the aircraft. Mounting the machine is easy if you are ex-Cavalry, but for mere mortals it can be quite an effort. Stepping over the left hand exhaust pipe, using the foot hold positioned some three feet from the cockpit, I clamber up and into the front cockpit and position myself on the wickerwork seat, which sits on the rear fuel tank!*

This rare colour photograph shows Lts Lew Potts and James H. Traill of No 1 Squadron discussing their reconnaissance flight in front of Bristol F2B A7194 at El Mejdel aerodrome, Palestine, in February 1918.
*via the Author*

## KNIGHTS OF THE AIR

### Andrew Edward McKeever

Born in Lostowel, Ontario, on 21 August 1894, Andrew Edward McKeever entered the war as a member of the Canadian Expeditionary Force, gaining a reputation as a marksman in the trenches until December 1916, when he transferred to the RFC. He was posted to No 11 Squadron on 28 May 1917, just as the unit was exchanging its FE2bs for F2Bs. McKeever's first claim, with 2Lt E Oake as his observer, was over two Albatros DVs on 26 June, but his back-seater in the next – over three DVs on 7 July – was 21-year-old 2Lt Leslie Archibald Powell, who would figure in the majority of his successes thereafter. Undoubtedly McKeever and Powell enjoyed their finest moment on 30 November 1917, as McKeever's DSO citation noted:

*'While on patrol by himself over enemy lines in very bad weather, he encountered two enemy two-seater machines and seven scouts. By skilful manoeuvring, he engaged one two-seater and destroyed it. As he turned to get back to the lines, five of the enemy dived on his tail, and his observer engaged and destroyed two of them. After an indecisive combat with two others, he attacked and destroyed one of the enemy which had overshot him. He continued the fight with the remainder until he was within 20ft of the ground, when the enemy machines climbed and left him.'* This combat brought McKeever's total to 31 and Powell's to 19, making him the highest scoring F2 pilot.

McKeever survived the war, but died on Christmas Day 1919 from injuries sustained in a car accident.

*via the Author*

Russell Smith © 2003 ASAA

'Settling into the cockpit, the first thing I am struck by is the fact that the overall view for the pilot is not very good. Indeed, the only view really on offer is the one straight ahead – ideal for sighting the forward-firing Vickers gun.

'Prior to starting the engine I first have to pressurise the fuel tanks, which is done by a hand pump on the left side of the cockpit. It is now time to prime the Falcon – 12 times on the priming pump when cold or eight when hot. The engine usually starts without a problem, and once it is running I leave it idling at 1,000rpm.

'The takeoff itself is a very gentle affair, as with very little effort the aircraft literally levitates off the ground in approximately 150 yards even without the assistance of a headwind. Once in flight, it soon becomes apparent that the F2B suffers from very heavy ailerons at speeds above 90mph. Associated adverse aileron yaw is also prevalent, whilst the rudder becomes ineffective near the stall.'

Landing the F2B can be tricky too, as Stuart Goldspink explained:

'On the approach to land you have to be careful to keep the engine warm by closing the coolant gills. A speed of 65-70mph must be maintained and the aircraft has to be landed INTO wind. The aircraft will not accept even a five-knot crosswind. The F2B settles in a three-point attitude on landing, and in calm wind conditions it has a tendency to ground loop in either direction.'

## TWO BIRDS WITH ONE STONE

'Two Birds with One Stone' depicts an engagement on 6 September 1918, in which Capt H. P. Lale and 2/Lt H. L. Edwards achieved simultaneous victories against Fokker D.VIIs while flying Bristol fighter E2181. Lale's combat report reads as follows: *'One Fokker Biplane passed within 30 yards of Bristol Fighter E2181. Capt Lale put about 50 rounds into it and sent it down in flames. The observer (2/Lt Edwards) was in the meantime firing with double Lewis gun at another E.A. about 40 yards away on the left. This E.A. first spun, then appeared to gain control, but a few seconds later burst into flames.'* Painting by Russell Smith

# IN COMBAT

A line-up of pilots and observers from No 22 Squadron on 1 April 1918. Leading aces included in this group are: fifth from left, 2Lt George Searle Lomax Hayward (24); eighth from left, Capt W. F. J. Harvey (26); and twelfth from left, Capt John E. Gurdon (28).
*via the Author*

NO 48 SQUADRON was the first unit to receive the F2A. On 5 April 1917 the squadron was led aloft on its first offensive patrol by Capt W. Leefe Robinson VC.

Much has been made of the disaster that followed over Douai, but it was very much a unique circumstance. Ignoring the higher speed and greater manoeuvrability that the F2A offered over other Allied two-seaters, Robinson adhered to the standard tactic of closing up the flight when attacked so that the rear gunners could provide each other with mutual support. He also disregarded advice not to fly at the low altitude of 4,000ft. On top of that, Robinson reportedly learned that the lubricating oil in the machine guns froze at high altitude. His solution was to stop oiling the guns. As the Bristols neared Arras at 11.00hrs, they were intercepted by five Albatros DIIIs of Jasta 11 lead by Oblt Manfred Freiherr von Richthofen. As the Germans closed in on the formation, Robinson's Bristols closed up, their gunners waiting for the enemy to come within range. The Albatros scouts bore

in fast, twin machine guns blazing, and almost immediately F2A A3340 fell out of formation and was forced down. The Bristol gunners did their best to engage their darting assailants, only to find their weapons seizing up and falling silent. By the time the action had ended four F2As had been brought down, leaving just two to limp home full of holes.

The shock defeat of No 48 Squadron's F2As could easily have spelt the end for the Bristol Fighter, however frontline pilots took matters into their own hands and hastily changed their tactics by flying the aircraft like a single-seater and using the Fighter's fixed forward-firing gun more offensively.

One of the first victories in the Fighter was claimed on 26 June 1917 by Canadian pilot Lt Andrew McKeever, who used the new tactics to hit an Albatros DV head-on. By the time McKeever was posted back to England at year-end he had been credited with the destruction of 31 aircraft (eight of which fell to his observer, Sgt L A Powell). This tally made the Canadian the leading Bristol, Fighter ace.

The upturn in the F2's fortunes convinced the War Office to equip all of its fighter-reconnaissance squadrons with the aircraft. By July 1918 19 units had been equipped with the F2B. Some 2,867 F 2Bs had been completed by Bristol and four sub-contractors by Armistice Day.

## ACES

German pilots soon grew wary of the formidable F2B once units employed more aggressive tactics, choosing to engage the Fighter only when the odds were seemingly in their favour. Nevertheless, pilots like McKeever (31 victories), S. F. H. Thompson (30 victories), A. C. Atkey (29 victories), J. E. Gurdon (28 victories) and D. Latimer (28 victories) all claimed high scores. Indeed, no fewer than 121 pilots and 126 observers claimed five or more victories in the F2.

# RAF SE5

**UNDOUBTEDLY ONE OF** the best British fighters of World War One, the SE5a was easily the most successful aircraft designed by the Royal Aircraft Factory (RAF). Although less nimble than its frontline contemporary, the Sopwith Camel, the SE5a could out-dive and out-climb the Camel, sustain more combat damage and yet remain intact despite performing high-g manoeuvres. The aircraft's only failing was centred on its original powerplant, the Hispano-Suiza 8A engine, which suffered from chronic unreliability.

The SE5a reached the Royal Flying Corps (RFC) in June 1917, and it soon became a firm favourite amongst the leading British and Empire aces of World War One. Indeed, men such as James McCudden, Mick Mannock, Anthony Beauchamp Proctor and George McElroy would all claim more then 40 aerial victories with the SE5/5a.

A sight dreaded by German pilots over the Western Front in 1917-18, the angular shape of the SE5a.
*John Dibbs/The Plane Picture Co*

long with the Sopwith Camel, the RAF SE5/5a was the best British fighter built during World War One. Their development ran in parallel to the point where the prototypes flew within five weeks of one another. However, unlike the squat, light and agile Camel, the SE5 was rakish, angular and heavy in comparison. Yet the latter machine's tractability meant that it was much easier to fly than the Camel, dived and climbed faster and could withstand severe battle damage.

Royal Aircraft Factory engineers John Kenworthy, Henry P. Folland and Maj Frank W. Goodden designed the SE5 around the brilliant new Hispano-Suiza 8A V8 engine, the RFC requesting that the scout be robustly built and capable of being flown safely by pilots of limited experience.

Even while the AIRCO DH2 pusher scout was helping to end the 'Fokker Scourge' by countering Germany's first fighters with synchronised machine guns in the summer of 1916, the RFC was aware of the ultimate superiority in performance that tractor biplanes such as the Bristol and Sopwith Scouts had over a pusher. The latter design would always be hampered by its drag-producing latticework structure of struts and wires that held the empennage aft of the engine and propeller. By the time the RFC received its first SPAD VII to evaluate on 9 September 1916, the RAF at Farnborough was engaged in designing its own Hispano-Suiza-powered fighter with a synchronised forward-firing machine gun.

In fact, Kenworthy, Folland and Goodden already had two ideas in the works as early as June of that year. One, was designated the SE5 (Scouting Experimental, No 5), which featured an engine in front and the pilot seated aft of the

*Top right:* **SE5as under construction at the Wolseley factory in Birmingham in 1918. No fewer than 5,125 SE5/5as were built in just 18 months by five companies in the UK.** *via Aviation-images.com*

*Below:* **The spotless Shuttleworth SE5a is the only original SE5a still airworthy.** *John Dibbs/The Plane Picture Co*

wings – essentially a smaller, more compactly proportioned single-seat version of the BE2c.

When the first 21 French-made Hispano-Suiza 8A engines were delivered to the RFC on 20 September 1916, most were slated for installation in license-built SPAD VIIs, but two were used to power the first and second SE5 prototypes, A4561 and A4562. On 28 November the RAF received its first example of the new geared 200hp Hispano-Suiza 8B, which it subsequently installed in the third prototype, A4563, thereby creating the first SE5a.

Tragically SE5 A4562 broke up during a test flight on 28 January 1917, killing Maj Goodden. Simple modifications corrected the aeroplane's structural problems, however, and the first production SE5, A4845, cleared its final inspection on 2 March 1917. The first production batch of SE5s did not make a promising impression on their pilots, who complained of

poor lateral control – a shortcoming that was alleviated somewhat, but never entirely, by shortening the wingspan and reducing the rake of the wingtips in later production SE5s and SE5as. Engine reduction and gun synchronisation problems also afflicted early SE5s. However, the Wolseley-developed direct-drive Viper engine proved to be the fighter's saviour, and this 200hp motor was installed in most SE5as.

Unlike the Camel, the SE5 proved to be a forgiving aeroplane that was tolerant of inexperienced pilots. Light on the controls and with innocuous stalling characteristics, the fighter was usefully manoeuvrable yet stable enough for the pilot to shoot accurately at his target. The SE5 was also solidly built, which meant that it could be thrown around the sky during a dogfight without its pilot having to fear the onset of structural failure. It is unsurprising, therefore, that the SE5a was the mount of most of the RFC's leading aces.

## NO 56 SQUADRON was the first unit

to receive SE5s, being issued with aircraft at London Colney in March 1917. One outstanding feature of the new fighter was a large 'half-glasshouse', which encircled half of the forward cockpit area. It was not liked by service pilots, however, who thought it cumbersome and a danger to the man in the cockpit in the event of a crash. Although authority was loath to have it removed, No 56 Squadron CO Maj R. G. Blomfield DSO discarded the 'glasshouse' in favour of a more standard windshield once his unit got to France.

Amongst the first pilots to fly the SE5 was 32-victory ace Capt Albert Ball, an eccentric but brilliantly aggressive loner whose exploits as a Nieuport pilot in No 60 Squadron were already legendary in the RFC. Ball had high expectations for the SE5, but after giving the first prototype a 10-minute test flight on 23 November 1916 he remarked with bitter regret that the new scout had 'turned out a dud'. Ball made no secret of his dislike for the SE5, and when the RFC's commander Maj Gen Hugh Trenchard, visited No 56 Squadron's sector in France, the ace entreated him to replace the new fighters with Nieuports.

Nevertheless, by then he had already taken the liberty of modifying his personal machine while waiting for No 56 Squadron's disembarkation orders at London Colney in March. He replaced the 'half-glasshouse' with a small Avro windscreen. He removed the adjustable armoured seat and replaced it with a board until a simpler seat could be installed. The lower slide on the Lewis' Foster mount was lengthened by two inches to make it easier for the pilot to replace the ammunition drums, and Ball discarded his synchronised Vickers gun entirely. He also removed the petrol and water gravity tanks from the upper wing and installed long SPAD-type exhaust pipes to the engine. Ball noted that his alterations resulted

in a considerable improvement in performance, although he still considered the SE5 to be 'a rotten machine'. The RAF adopted many of the ace's revisions for future production aircraft, and the SE5 was the better for it. The undercarriage wheels were also moved farther forward and the external overwing tank replaced by internally fitted fuel and water gravity tanks behind the leading edge of the upper wing centre section. The latter was also strengthened and covered with plywood to withstand the Lewis gun's recoil.

The subsequent replacement of the SE5's 150hp Hispano-Suiza with a more powerful 200hp model, along with further refinements, produced the SE5a, the first of which began arriving at No 56 Squadron in June 1917. Fast, rugged and almost viceless, the SE5a became a mainstay of the RFC and later of the RAF over the Western Front right up to the end of the war. The first unit to employ it, 'Fighting Fifty-Six', was also the most successful, being credited with 401 victories by the end of the war, and producing numerous famous aces, two of whom – Albert Ball and James Thomas Byford McCudden – were awarded Britain's highest military decoration, the Victoria Cross (VC).

No 74 Squadron's B Flight line up at Clairmarais North in the late summer of 1918. SE5a '2' was assigned to Capt Keith 'Grid' Caldwell (25 victories). *via Aviation-images.com*

## CUSTOMISING THE SE5

Seen here with Capt Albert Ball in the cockpit and the Lewis gun carried on the upper-wing centre section pulled back to fire obliquely forward and upward in the fashion much favoured by the RFC's then leading ace, this SE5 (A8907) has the original type of semi-cockpit transparency that was disliked by virtually all pilots and soon removed in favour of a small windscreen. *via Aviation-images.com*

# FROM THE COCKPIT

UNLIKE ITS GREAT rival the Camel, the SE5/5a had none of the Sopwith's scout's lack of stability and waspish sensitivity that were assets in the hands of a competent pilot and potentially fatal to the novice. The RAF fighter, by contrast, was a compromise between agility and tractability, proving to be a forgiving aeroplane that was tolerant of mishandling by inexperienced pilots. Control forces about all three axes were light, and although there was some adverse aileron yaw, its stalling characteristics were totally innocuous.

Capt James McCudden of No 56 Squadron was one of only two pilots to claim more than 50 victories with the SE5/5a, and he commented favourably on the machine in his diary following his first patrol in one in July 1917:

## 'THE SE5 WAS A MOST EFFICIENT FIGHTING MACHINE' Capt James McCudden

'We crossed the lines at 16,000 ft over Dixmude. This was the first time I had ever been in an SE5, and although it felt rather strange, I liked the machine immensely, as it was very fast after the Sopwith Scout (Pup), and one could see out of it so thoroughly well.

'The SE5 was a most efficient fighting machine – far and away superior to the enemy machines of that period. It had a Vickers gun shooting forward through the propeller, and a Lewis gun shooting forward over the top plane, parallel to the Vickers, but above the propeller. The pilot could also incline the Lewis gun upwards in such a way that he could shoot vertically upwards at a target that presented itself.

'Other good points of the SE5 were its strength, its diving and zooming powers and its splendid view. Apart from this, it was most warm, comfortable and an easy machine to fly.'

Capt Cecil Lewis claimed eight victories while flying with No 56 Squadron alongside Maj McCudden, and he praised the scout in his book 'Farewell to Wings':

'By the summer of 1917, the SE5 was a formidable opponent for any German fighter. It could be dived to terminal velocity without breaking up. It had no vices and would spin left and right without being difficult to pull out, as some other aircraft were. It was easy to land and had a broad, strong undercarriage.

'The SE5 was probably the first fighting aircraft to be produced which was both reliable enough and steady enough to stand up to the rough and tumble of 30 or 40 aircraft milling around trying to shoot each other down. In such conditions, pilots did not think much about "handling". They were pretty rough on the controls. Slammed into a dive, yanked into climb, pulled hard round in a split-arse turn, the aircraft structure had to stand up to enormous and sudden strains. The SE5 came through this ordeal triumphantly, and justified the belief of the top brass that it would give the Allies the supremacy of the air in 1917. It did.'

*Top:* **An SE5a of B Flight, No 32 Squadron, provides a willing target for British anti-aircraft gunners practicing their 'art' on the Western Front in 1918.**
*via Aviation-images.com*

*Right:* **Lt Robert Allan 'Bloody Bobs' Caldwell of A Flight, No 56 Squadron, poses with his SE5a at Bethencourt.**
*via Aviation-images.com*

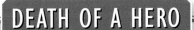

# DEATH OF A HERO

Albert Ball is known to history as one of the most beloved British aces of all time. Though typically quiet and introverted on the ground, he was a skillful and aggressive pilot in the air. His death, late in the afternoon of 7 May 1917, was a blow to the morale of the British airmen. According to eyewitness accounts, the weather in the area started out fine, but as the afternoon progressed rain and thunderstorms moved into the area. Despite the diminishing weather, a number of patrols were made that day which were marked by several encounters with German Albatrosses. Late in the afternoon, 10 pilots (including Albert Ball) of No 56 Squadron took off on another patrol. Germans were spotted again and chaos ensued resulting in the pilots losing track of each other in the air. After some confusion, Cyril Crowe spotted Albert Ball nearby and turned to follow him. Crowe reports that he then saw Ball fire two red Very lights to indicate that he had seen enemy aircraft and was turning to engage them, although he added that he himself could not immediately see the German aircraft.

Ball did, however, engage an Albatros which evidence suggests was being flown by Lothar von Richthofen. Crowe watched as Ball pursued the Albatros into a cumulus cloud. From there the eyewitness accounts shift to the ground. Four Germans reported seeing Albert Ball emerge from the clouds at a very low altitude and inverted. They watched as Ball's SE5 crashed to the ground. A young French girl was the first to reach the scene and she removed Ball's body from the wreckage. Ball was buried with honours by his German adversaries and was posthumously awarded the Victoria Cross. Although Lothar von Richthofen was credited with the victory, debate still persists as to whether Ball's death can be attributed to Lothar or simply a case of vertigo brought on while flying through a cloud. *Painting by Russell Smith*

# FACT FILE

# CONSTRUCTION

### COCKPIT

RAF engineers made a serious attempt to organise a functional instrument panel. This saw oil temperature, oil pressure and radiator temperature gauges grouped near the altimeter, airspeed indicator and compass on the right side of the instrument panel.

### ENGINE

The key to the success of the SE5/5a was its V8 liquid-cooled engine, initially in the form of the direct-drive 150hp Hispano-Suiza 8A. After 77 SE5s had been built with this powerplant, production switched to the SE5a, which was fitted with the geared 200hp Hispano-Suiza 8B engine. Production of this engine under licence by Wolseley Motors Ltd initially proved problematic due to unreliability. Things only started to improve when Wolseley modified a 150hp engine into the high-compression, direct-drive W4A Viper of 200hp. This engine was vastly superior increasing the SE5a's top speed by a full 7mph and improving its rate of climb.

### FUSELAGE

For ease of manufacture, the SE5/5a featured a box-girder fuselage made up from ash longerons and spruce spacers, the whole structure being wire-braced, fabric-covered and surmounted by curved decking formed by stringers. A headrest fairing was soon fitted to the fuselage decking immediately aft of the cockpit, although some pilots chose to have this removed in the field.

### TAIL

Like the fuselage, ash woodwork was used in the main to form the structure of the fin, rudder, tailplanes and elevators, all of which were covered in fabric. The aeroplane's tailskid was somewhat unusual, however, for it was steerable.

### WINGS

The single-bay, staggered wings of parallel chord were built around two spruce spars with internal wire bracing, and with ailerons on upper and lower wings. Following the crash of the second prototype SE5, which was almost certainly caused by wing structure failure during aerobatics, the RAF modified the design to incorporate strengthened rear spars, shortened wings with reduced rake and strengthened strut/spar joints.

### ARMAMENT

The SE5 was the first British single-seat fighter to mount two machine guns. The RAF combined a synchronised Vickers machine gun in the fuselage with a Lewis firing over the propeller arc by means of a Foster mount on the upper wing. The 0.303in Vickers gun was enclosed in the left fuselage and was synchronised to fire 400 rounds of belt-fed ammunition through the propeller. The 0.303in Lewis gun on a Foster mounting above the upper wing could be pulled down for reloading.

SE5a B4891 of Capt
J. T. B. McCudden,
No 56 Squadron, Baizieux,
France, February 1918.
*Courtesy Osprey Publishing*

## SPECIFICATIONS

### RAF SE5a

| | |
|---|---|
| **Engine:** | Wolseley W4a Viper |
| **Power:** | 215hp |
| **Max Speed:** | 138mph (222km/h) |
| **Length:** | 20ft 11in (6.37m) |
| **Wingspan:** | 26ft 7.5in (8.11m) |
| **Height:** | 9ft 6in (2.89m) |
| **Armament:** | One fixed 0.303in Vickers machine guns and one 0.303in Lewis machine gun on Foster mount |
| **Max all-up weight:** | 1,976lb (896kg) |
| **Range:** | 300 miles (483km) |
| **Number built:** | 5,125 |
| **Entered service:** | March 1917 |

| 1916 | 1917 | | |
|---|---|---|---|
| **22 November:** Maj Frank W. Goodden flies the prototype SE5 A4561. | **28 January:** Maj Frank W. Goodden killed in the second SE5 prototype A4562. | **March:** No 56 Squadron equipped with the first SE5s. | **22 April:** First SE5 combat sortie. |

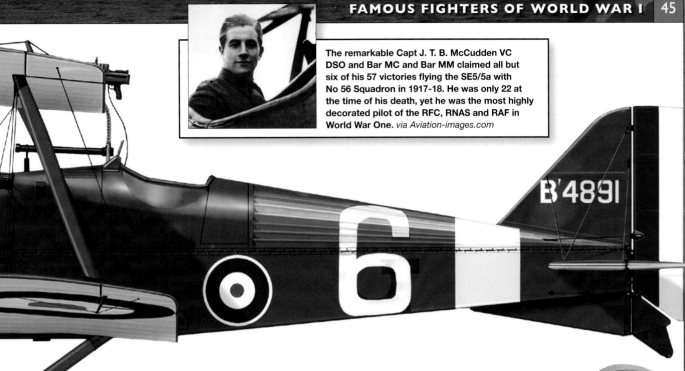

The remarkable Capt J. T. B. McCudden VC DSO and Bar MC and Bar MM claimed all but six of his 57 victories flying the SE5/5a with No 56 Squadron in 1917-18. He was only 22 at the time of his death, yet he was the most highly decorated pilot of the RFC, RNAS and RAF in World War One. *via Aviation-images.com*

B'4891

6

Luigino Caliaro

IN CLOSE-UP

John Dibbs/The Plane Picture Co

Luigino Caliaro

## DID YOU KNOW?

- Unlike many of its contemporaries, which were armed with twin belt-fed synchronised machine guns, the SE5 was fitted with one synchronised Vickers 0.303in machine gun immediately forward of the cockpit and a similar calibre Lewis gun on a Foster mounting firing over the upper wing.

- Co-designer of the SE5, Maj Frank W Goodden, made the fighter's first flight (in A4561) on 22 November 1917. 'Its's a pixie!' he declared to Henry P. Folland after landing.

- By the end of World War One, 2,765 SE5/5as had been built, and some 2,500 more would be completed before production ceased in 1919.

- A handful of squadrons saw action with the SE5a away from the Western Front, fighting German, Turkish and Austro-Hungarian units in the Middle East and the Balkans.

- The only Australian-manned SE5a unit was No 2 Squadron, Australian Flying Corps (AFC), which began receiving the new aircraft as replacements for its DH5s in January 1918. No fewer than 14 pilots would 'make ace' whilst serving with this unit on the Western Front.

- No fewer than 5,125 SE5/5as were built in just 18 months and these were issued to 22 British and American squadrons on the Western Front.

| **3 April:** | **7 May:** | **August:** | **1918** | | **July:** | **8-10 August:** | **1920** |
| | | | **19 June:** | | | | **January:** |
| Capt Albert Ball scores the first E5 victories. | Capt Albert Ball killed in action in SE5 A4850. | First Wolseley W4a Viper engines produced, which will eclipse the Hispano-Suiza in SE5as. | Ranking British and Empire ace Maj 'Billy' Bishop claims his final five victories in less than 15 minutes while flying an SE5s with No 84 Squadron. |  | No 92 Squadron becomes the last SE5a unit sent to France to fight on the Western Front. | Battle of Amiens, which sees SE5as and Sopwith Camels numerically dominate the RAF inventory. | RAF withdraws the last SE5as from service. |

# IN COMBAT

THE FIRST SE5s to be issued to a frontline unit were delivered to No 56 Squadron at London Colney, near St Albans, in mid-March 1917. Following training on the aircraft, the unit flew to Vert Galant, in France, on 7 April. The SE5 conducted its first patrol 15 days later, and on 23 April Capt Albert Ball claimed the aeroplane's first victory when he downed an Albatros D III scout.

Altogether, some 16 units were supposed to have been flying the aircraft by December, but in reality only Nos 24, 32, 40, 41, 56, 60 and 84 Squadrons had received SE5as because of the aforementioned unreliability issues. However, by the spring of 1918 most of the technical maladies that had beset the SE5a were now behind it, and the aircraft was now considered to be the best British fighter of the day. It was

**These SE5as of No 85 Squadron were built under sub-contract and have had their serial numbers deleted by the censor – note that none of them have headrests.**
*via Aviation-images.com*

faster, though less manoeuvrable, than the Camel, though the latter was also superior as a ground attack platform thanks to the pilot's seating position further forward.

With the Camel revelling in medium to low altitude combat, the SE5a was left to hold its own at higher ceilings. Fortunately for the RFC and, from 1 April 1918, the Royal Air Force (RAF), the SE5a was the superior aircraft at altitudes exceeding 10,000ft in any case. Therefore, squadrons equipped with the fighter tended to be used more for aerial combat at medium to high altitudes, and much less in the air-to-ground role. Furthermore, the SE5a's armament of one forward-firing Vickers machine gun in front of the pilot and a single Lewis gun affixed to the top wing made the aircraft ideal for stalking high-flying prey. Pilots could sneak up beneath a hostile machine, ratchet down the gun and fire up into the underbelly of the enemy aircraft.

Some of the best-known pilots of the RFC and RAF scored the majority of their victories in the SE5/5a. The leading British and Empire ace of the war, Lt Col 'Billy' Bishop, scored 36 of his 72 victories in the SE5/5a, Capt Anthony Beauchamp Proctor claimed all 54 of his in the aircraft while Maj James McCudden was credited with 51 victories in the SE5a from a total of 57. No fewer than 92 pilots claimed ten or more victories with the SE5/5a, and a good number of these men achieved high scores.

The vast majority of these pilots claimed their successes over the Western Front against a wide range of German fighter types. However, six of them were serving with units in Macedonia (Nos 17, 47 and 150 Squadrons) and Palestine (Nos 111 and 145 Squadrons). In the latter theatre, SE5as were heavily engaged during Gen Sir Edmund Allenby's final offensive in the late summer of 1918, the aircraft performing both ground attack sorties (using 20lb Cooper bombs) and patrols over enemy aerodromes.

## KNIGHTS OF THE AIR

### Anthony F. W. Beauchamp Proctor

Born on 4 September 1894, Anthony Beauchamp Proctor was recruited into the RFC in March 1917 and joined No 84 Squadron in late July, just as the unit received the first of its SE5as. Heading to France with the squadron, he failed to score his first victory until 3 January 1918.

Due to his modest height (he was just over five foot tall), Beauchamp Proctor had to have the rudder pedals and seat fitted in his fighter adjusted so that he could reach them.

Despite his low-key start in terms of aerial successes, Beauchamp Proctor quickly hit his straps from February onwards. By mid June he had claimed 12 aircraft and four kite balloons destroyed, and 12 more aircraft sent down out of control. Beauchamp Proctor continued to add to his tally of victories until he suffered severe wounds in his forearm on 8 October that forced him to be hospitalised until March 1919. His final tally stood at 54 victories, of which 16 were tethered observation kite balloons. Beauchamp Proctor received the DSO and VC whilst convalescing in hospital, which he added to his MC and DFC. Granted a permanent commission in the RAF in 1920, he joined No 24 Squadron shortly afterwards. However, on 21 June 1921 Beauchamp Proctor was killed in a flying accident whilst practising aerobatics in a Sopwith Snipe for the forthcoming Hendon Air Pageant.

**Capt A. F. W. Beauchamp Proctor, No 84 Squadron, Bertangles, France, August 1918.**
*via the author*

Like the Camel, the SE5a did not survive long in the peacetime RAF, with the last aircraft being withdrawn from Nos 56 and 81 Squadrons in January 1920. Small numbers remained in service in Canada and Australia, however, and more than 60 SE5as were built from components in the USA in 1919. These served as the US Army's frontline fighter force until indigenous types entered service in the early 1920s.

**Capt Benjamin 'Dad' Roxburgh-Smith claimed 22 victories with the SE5a whilst serving with No 74 Squadron's B Flight between April and October 1918.**
*via Aviation-images.com*

## ACES

The SE5/5a was, along with the Camel, the major British fighting scout of the last 18 months of the war in France. It equipped several major units, the first being No 56 Squadron in March 1917. This unit became famous for the number of aces it had among its pilots, including Albert Ball, James McCudden, Geoffrey Bowman, Richard Maybery, Leonard Barlow, Hank Burden and Cyril Crowe. In all, 26 aces flew the aircraft with No 56 Squadron alone. Other well known units were Nos 1, 24, 29, 32, 40, 41, 60, 64, 2 AFC, 74, 84, 85 and 92 Squadrons. A number of VC winners also flew SE5/5as too, namely Ball, Mannock, McCudden, Beauchamp Proctor and Bishop – all high-scoring aces. Of the 217 pilots who 'made ace' with the SE5/5a, no fewer than 20 scored more than 20 victories.

John Dibbs/The Plane Picture Co

# SURVIVORS

## ALTHOUGH OVER FIVE

thousand SE5/5as were constructed, only five original examples are known to have survived. Three of these are resident in the UK, these aircraft having once formed part of Maj John Savage's 45-strong fleet of SE5as purchased post-war for commercial use such as skywriting and crop spraying. One of them (above) is maintained in airworthy condition by the Shuttleworth Collection. Bearing the civil registration G-EBIA, this aircraft was acquired by the Armstrong Whitworth company in the late 1930s. It remained in the company's flight shed at Whitley until bought

by the Shuttleworth Collection in 1955. It was restored at Farnborough in 1957-59, the fighter requiring an Hispano-Suiza engine, cowling, radiator and numerous other parts. Flown for the first time in more than 30 years on 4 August 1959, the aircraft has remained airworthy ever since.

Sister-aircraft G-EBIC was sold by Skywriters Ltd to G. R. Nash in 1937, the fighter becoming a part of the latter's collection of historic aeroplanes and vehicles. In 1955 it was sold to the Royal Aeronautical Society and was eventually taken on charge by the emergent RAF Museum at Hendon in March 1963.

The last of the three Skywriters Ltd aircraft to survive is G-EBIB. Upon its retirement in July 1939, the fighter was handed over to the Science Museum in South Kensington and was restored to a wartime appearance minus armament. It remained in this scheme for many years until restored to its former glory as G-EBIB in full Skywriters Ltd colours in the late 1990s.

## REPLICAS

A handful of accurate flying replicas also exist across the globe, with the most authentic being the trio of SE5as built by New Zealand-based The Vintage Aviator Ltd. These machines have been constructed using original RAF drawings. Fitted with reproduction Lewis and Vickers guns, the aircraft are powered by original Hispano-Suiza direct-drive 180hp V8 engines.

# ALBATROS D.V

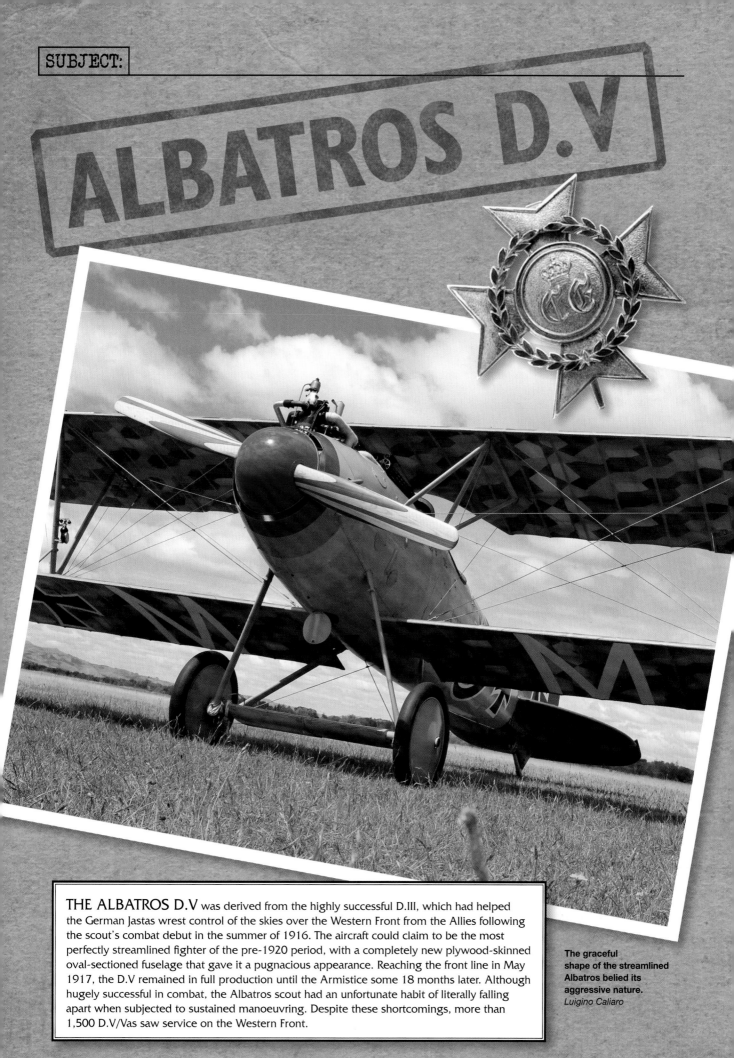

THE ALBATROS D.V was derived from the highly successful D.III, which had helped the German Jastas wrest control of the skies over the Western Front from the Allies following the scout's combat debut in the summer of 1916. The aircraft could claim to be the most perfectly streamlined fighter of the pre-1920 period, with a completely new plywood-skinned oval-sectioned fuselage that gave it a pugnacious appearance. Reaching the front line in May 1917, the D.V remained in full production until the Armistice some 18 months later. Although hugely successful in combat, the Albatros scout had an unfortunate habit of literally falling apart when subjected to sustained manoeuvring. Despite these shortcomings, more than 1,500 D.V/Vas saw service on the Western Front.

The graceful shape of the streamlined Albatros belied its aggressive nature.
*Luigino Caliaro*

Domination of the skies over the Western Front by German fighters tended to ebb and flow depending on the quality of the aircraft being fielded. For the first three years of the conflict, the Allies tended to play catch up as fighting scouts from Fokker, Halberstadt and Albatros proved superior to the designs being flown by British and French units. In an effort to counter the 'Fokker Scourge', the British developed pusher scouts such as the DH2 and the French opted for elegant tractor fighters from Nieuport. By the time the Battle of the Somme

DIII engine and had a semi-monocoque wooden fuselage that differed radically from the fabric-skinned, braced box-girder type fuselages then in almost universal use. Aside from its revolutionary monocoque structure, the D.I was also fitted with two 7.92mm Maxim 08/15 machine guns – the first fighter produced in quantity to boast two such weapons.

The Albatros D.I was not as agile as its principal Allied opponents, but it soon won pilots over thanks to its superior speed and firepower. Aviators were less than enthusiastic about the upward vision from the cockpit,

## 'THEIR CLIMB RATE AND MANOEUVRABILITY ARE ASTONISHING' Leutnant Erwin Böhme, Jasta 2

commenced on 1 July 1916, Allied fighters had virtually re-taken command of the sky.

Stung into action, German aircraft designers were strongly influenced by the Nieuport 17 and Sopwith Scout (better known as the Pup) that were now appearing in increasing numbers over the front lines. Aiding the cause of aircraft manufacturers in Germany was the development of the Mercedes DIII six-cylinder inline water-cooled engine, which had double the power of the 80hp Oberursel rotary engine that had previously been the motor of choice for Idflieg scouts.

Amongst the crop of new scouts developed in the spring of 1916 was the debut fighter design from the Albatros Werke of Johannisthal. This machine, created by Robert Thelen, featured a

however, complaining that both the upper wing and the trestle-type centre-section struts blocked their view. Thelen duly lowered the upper wing and fitted N-shaped cabane struts, splayed outward. The modified aircraft was designated the D.II.

The arrival of the Albatros D.I/II in the front line in the autumn of 1916 coincided with a radical re-organisation of the German fighter force. Specialised fighter squadrons known as Jagdstaffeln had begun to form in August of that year, and their primary aim was to gain local air superiority over 'hot spots'. This was achieved through the implementation of new tactics that suited the fast, heavy-hitting, Albatros and Halberstadt fighters that were now entering service in significant numbers.

*Undoubtedly the most authentic reproduction Albatros D.Va in the world today is the aircraft built by New Zealand-based The Vintage Aviator Ltd (TVAL), which flew for the first time in late 2009. Powered by a Mercedes DIIIa engine, the aircraft is marked up as D.Va D.5284/17 of Jasta 5's Vizefeldwebel Josef Mai.*
*Luigino Caliaro*

Keen to build on the success of the D.I/II, and inspired by the fighters' French Nieuport 17 rival, the Albatros design team adopted the latter machine's sesquiplane wing arrangement. The result featured two wings with a long curving rake at the tips, the lower of which was of considerably reduced chord. These in turn provided a superior downward view for the pilot, and gave the D.III improved manoeuvrability and a better rate of climb than the D.II. Idflieg duly ordered 400 examples in October 1916. Reaching front-line units from late December 1916, the new machine quickly proved rather fragile in combat, and a series of structural failures saw the aircraft grounded.

## THE FOLLOW-ON D.V had by now

commenced flight-testing, this aircraft being even more streamlined than the sleek D.III. Again featuring a sesquiplane wing layout, but with gap between the upper and lower flying surfaces reduced by 110cm, the scout featured an elliptical cross-section fuselage, a fully enclosed cowling, a more rounded rudder profile and an altered tailskid. Strangely, considering its previous D.III experience, Idflieg's engineers tested the new aeroplane's fuselage and rudder but failed to static-test the wings before ordering 200 D.Vs. The first examples began arriving at the front in May, and almost from the outset reports came in of wingtip flutter and structural failure. The lightened fuselage structure also proved to be prone to cracking during rough landings, resulting in the aircraft literally breaking up.

Despite the fighter's worrying structural problems, construction of the D.V continued because of the tremendous demand for Albatros scouts. The Albatros Werke, which had an impressive production capacity of 190 airframes per month, had by then geared up for the production of the D.V and enjoyed something of a monopoly at this time. Albatros duly embarked upon a structural reappraisal, the end result of which was the D.Va, which featured stronger wing spars, heavier ribs and additional fuselage members.

In the spring of 1918, Albatros aircraft (and specifically the D.V/Va) remained the most numerically important fighters available when the Germans launched their final offensive of World War One on 21 March 1918. And in spite of the scout's shortcomings, German tactics and piloting skill meant that the Albatros D.Va remained a dangerous foe that Allied aviators dismissed at their peril.

*Top:* **The prototype Albatros D.V had its wings, rudder and tailplane covered in five-colour printed 'lozenge' camouflage fabric. Unusually, this was also applied to the plywood-covered fuselage.**
*via Aviation-images.com*

*Above:* **Seven-victory ace Vizefeldwebel Karl Friedrich Kurt Jentsch is seen in the cockpit of his Jasta 61 Albatros D.Va D.2343/17 during the summer of 1918.**
*via Aviation-images.com*

*Left:* **Albatros D.Vs and D.IIIs, and an AEG C.IV 'hack', of Jasta 12 are seen lined up for the camera at Roucourt in the late summer of 1917. The first two D.Vs were assigned to eight-victory ace, Ltn d R Viktor Schobinger.**
*via Aviation-images.com*

# FROM THE COCKPIT

ALL ALBATROS FIGHTERS were fairly easy aircraft to fly in comparison with other scouts of the period such as the Fokker DrI and Sopwith Camel. Less agile than most of their contemporaries, the strengths of the D.I/II in particular lay in their high diving speed and mechanical reliability. Vizefeldwebel Carl Holler was an early Albatros pilot with Jasta 6, and he recalled: *'Its rate of climb was excellent – it was child's play to reach 5,000 metres. Because of its heavy in-line engine, it had a tremendous diving speed, which gave us great advantage when attacking the enemy flying below. Now we did not have to wait very long to obtain a few victories. In short order, one after another, two of my comrades each obtained a victory.'*

As previously mentioned, the follow-on D.III was very similar to the early Albatros types in all areas bar its wing planform. Responding to criticism that D.Is and D.IIs were being outmanoeuvred in aerial combat by the graceful Nieuport 11/17 (whose pilots also benefited from the French scout's superb field of view downward), Albatros embraced the sesquiplane wing layout. However, a fully loaded Nieuport 11 weighed a mere 480kg, while a similarly loaded Albatros D.III weighed in at 810kg!

Once in front-line use, the fragile lower wing proved unable to cope with the strains of combat. High-scoring ace Ernst Udet of Jasta 37 was fortunate enough to recognise a potential wing failure in his aircraft when chasing a French SPAD VII on 26 May 1917. *'I push down – I have to get him! But the wings of my Albatros are not up to the strain. They begin to flutter more and more, so that I fear the machine will disintegrate in the air. I give up*

as 18 July, Rittmeister Manfred von Richthofen had written the following pointed note to his friend Oberleutnant Fritz von Falkenhayn, the Kogenluft (Commander-General of the air force) staff's technical officer: *'Our aircraft are laughingly inferior to the English. Their Triplane and 200hp SPAD, as well as the Sopwith single-seater (Camel), play with our D.Vs. Besides better quality, they also have superiority in numbers. All of our good fighter pilots are lost in this manner. The D.V is so obsolete and so ridiculously inferior to the English that one can't begin to do anything with his aircraft. But the people at home have not bought anything new for almost a year, except for this lousy Albatros, and have remained stuck with the D.III design. As long as Albatros has no energetic competition, we are left in the lurch with the D.III and D.V.'*

Manfred von Richthofen pinned his hopes on the Fokker DrI triplane. Due to its own disastrous wing failures, however, the DrI would not reach the front in quantity until January 1918. Albatros would remain the primary supplier of German fighter aircraft until then.

## DESPERATE MANOEUVRES

In the last week of August 1917 there was little aerial activity due to bad weather. For this reason, Albatros pilot Otto Fuchs made use of an afternoon free from rain and storm for an orientation flight in the area behind the front with pilots newly transferred to the Staffel, Lt Rudolf von der Horst and Lt Kurt Katzenstein. But, as he later related, things did not go quite as planned... *'When we had reached flight altitude it became more and more unpleasant. Heavy gusts of wind and an ever darkening sky heralded a strong summer storm. I became concerned about my two inexperienced pilots and decided to leave the altitude of about 3,000 meters and to return to Phalempin in a descending flight. Suddenly the black layer of clouds tore open, rays of sunlight shortly appeared, and I spotted a group of English fighter planes above us. From their superior position the Englishmen immediately went over to the attack and dove down upon us. Since I was flying higher than the two novices as protection, I was the first to be attacked by two Englishmen, and immediately let myself spin down. While the bank of clouds approached threateningly, I was forced down lower and lower by my pursuers. I attempted to evade my pursuers while under constant fire, finally at the height of the tree tops. Again and again strong gusts of wind shifted my Albatros over several meters, so that I was afraid of ramming into a tree or a building. My machine had already been hit several times, when suddenly a hazy wall of rain appeared before me. This was my salvation: I flew right into the wall of rain and immediately pulled the stick upwards in order not to crash into a tower or a tree. In the heavy rain shower I spotted a meadow below me and began to land. While doing so, my Albatros was pretty well wrecked.'*

When Otto Fuchs returned to Phalempin, soaked through and covered in mud, he discovered to his relief that his two comrades had also survived the air combat unharmed. *Painting by Russell Smith*

Three comrades from Jasta 'Boelcke' pose with an unidentified Albatros D.V from their unit probably in the late summer of 1917. They are, from left to right, Ltn Gerhard Bassenge (seven victories), Ltn d R Fritz Kempf (four victories) Ltn d R Hermann Vallendor (six victories).
*via Aviation-images.com*

*the chase and return home.'* And even after the D.V had been hastily strengthened and returned to production in D.Va form, pilots were advised not to over-dive their Albatros aircraft. Such a restriction had a terrible effect on pilot morale.

Nevertheless, by 31 August 1917 424 D.V fighters were recorded in the Frontbestand. Although many German pilots now realised these aircraft were inferior to the best Allied types, there were no others available. As early

Eight-victory SE5a ace Capt Cecil A. Lewis of No 56 Squadron flew a captured Albatros in June 1917, commenting: *'It was big and heavy. In fact the Germanic temperament showed up all along. The machine was sluggish, strong, reliable and determined. It had none of the feeling of lightness and grace that our aircraft had. To throw the Albatros around in the air was hard work, and it would have made you sweat in a dogfight'.*

# FACT FILE

## CONSTRUCTION

### COCKPIT

Featuring just two instruments (a tachometer and a fuel quantity gauge) and a compass, the cockpit was dominated by the fuel tank and ammunition belt container, which sat side-by-side. Sat on a bucket seat made of thin aluminium sheet covered with leatherette material, the pilot had a tubular steel control column and a rudder control bar. The primary engine throttle handle was attached to the left side of the control column, as were the triggers for the two machine guns.

### FUSELAGE

Dispensing with the flat-sided fuselage structure of the D.I/II/III, Albatros went for an elliptical cross-section instead. To achieve this, an additional spruce longeron was added to either side of the fighter's centreline.

### TAIL

The curved tail surfaces were built into the rear fuselage. The fixed surfaces were made of wood, while the upper and lower fin, which supported the ash tailskid, were covered in plywood skin. The tailplane was fabric-covered.

### WINGS

The D.III and the D.V shared the same sesquiplane wing design, Albatros designers drawing their inspiration for this layout from Nieuport scouts of the period. Both wings were fabric-covered wooden structures, with the top surface following the usual Albatros formula of two box-spars positioned well forward and with a wire trailing edge. Ailerons were of steel-tube framework.

### ARMAMENT

As with its predecessors since the D.I, the Albatros D.V was armed with twin 7.92mm LMG 08/15 machine guns with 500 rounds of ammunition each. Both the D.V's Hedke interrupter gear and the improved Semmler gear that synchronised the D.Va's guns were developed by Albatros factory Werkmeisters.

### UNDERCARRIAGE

A conventional streamline-section steel-tube vee-strut type undercarriage chassis was fitted to sockets mounted on the fuselage. A single spreader bar behind the axle tied the vees together. This structure provided the D.V with additional lift.

### ENGINE

All Albatros scouts were powered by the Mercedes DIII six-cylinder inline water-cooled engine, which had been too powerful for most aircraft when it was first introduced. Typical of German aero engines of the period, the DIII's six cylinders were positioned vertically, with a massive six-throw crankshaft running in plain bearings.

**1917**

**21 April:**
Albatros informs Idflieg of its 'lightened Albatros D.III airframe' and gets first order for 200 D.Vs.

**May:**
First Albatros D.Vs arrive at Jagstaffeln.

**23 June:**
Luftstreitkräfte inaugurates 'Amerikaprogramm', designed to double the number of front-line units.

**23 June:**
Rittmeiste Manfred Freiherr vo Richthofer claims his victory wi the D.V (h 54th in tot

## SPECIFICATIONS

### Albatros D.V

| | |
|---|---|
| Engine: | Mercedes DIIIa |
| Power: | 160hp |
| Max Speed: | 115mph (185km/h) |
| Length: | 24ft 2in (7.33m) |
| Wing span: | 29ft 8in (9.04m) |
| Height: | 8ft 10in (2.70m) |
| Armament: | Two 7.92mm Maxim LMG 08/15 'Spandau' machine guns |
| Max all-up weight: | 2,066lb (937kg) |
| Range: | 230 miles (368km) |
| Number built: | 900 D.Vs and 1,612 D.Vas |
| Entered service: | May 1917 |

**June:**
geschwader I, ned under meister Manfred herr von thofen and prising Jastas 10 and 11, is ed with D.Vs.

**18 July:**
von Richthofen writes to Idflieg denouncing D.V.

**August:**
Idflieg orders first 262 examples of new, strengthened Albatros D.Va.

**1918**

**21 March-5 April:**
German Kaiserschlacht offensive begins in Picardy with Operation 'Michael', and 928 D.Vas and 131 D.Vs form the bulk of the German fighter force.

**8-10 August:**
Battle of Amiens, with the Fokker D.VII as the principal German fighter. Albatros D.Va still serving a supplementary role, along with Pfalz D.IIIa and D XII, Roland D.VI and Siemens-Schukert D.III and D.IV.

**11 November:**
More than 150 D.Vas still serving as fighters when the Armistice comes into effect.

**Ltn d R Ernst Udet** (who survived the war with 62 victories, making him second only to von Richthofen and Germany's leading surviving ace) flew this black Albatros D.Va as commander of Jasta 37 in Flanders in late 1917-18. The unit markings consisted of the black fuselage and diagonal black/white stripes seen on the tailplane. Udet's famous personal **LO** (his nickname for his fiancé, Eleonore Zink) emblem can also seen on the fuselage. After long service the aircraft was written off in a crash landing. *Courtesy Osprey Publishing*

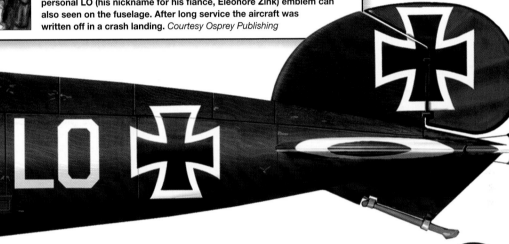

**IN CLOSE-UP**

*Luigino Caliaro*

*Luigino Caliaro*

## DID YOU KNOW?

- Albatros Werke was founded in 1910 at Johannisthal airfield, near Berlin, and initially licence-built French Farman type box kites and Gnome-engined Antoinette monoplanes.

- The 'D' in German fighter designations stood for Doppeldecker, or biplane.

- None of the Albatros scouts produced during World War One were as manoeuvrable as their French or British counterparts, but they usually had greater firepower and speed.

- The Albatros D.V, with its streamlined, elliptical cross-section fuselage and fully enclosed cowling, was the most aerodynamic fighter of World War One.

- Albatros received an order from Idflieg for 200 D.Vs in April 1917, these being officially referred to as 'lightened D.IIIs'. A further 400 were ordered the following month and 300 in July. Production of the aircraft then switched to the more robust D.Va.

- By 31 August 1917, Albatros products – 424 D.Vs, 385 D.IIIs and 56 D.I and IIs – made up 84 per cent of the 1,030 fighters in the German front-line inventory.

- Although described as a 'lightened Albatros D.III', the D.Va ended up being more than 100kg heavier than its predecessor following urgent wing strengthening after numerous in-flight structural failures.

# IN COMBAT

THE ALBATROS D.V was developed to counter the SE5s and SPAD VII/XIIIs that had started to achieve ascendancy over the D.III by mid-summer 1917. It quickly became clear to units equipped with the aircraft that the D.V did not have a sufficient increase in performance to restore the balance of power in their favour. Undeterred, Idflieg ordered that the fighter be built in large numbers in the hope that a significant force of Albatros scouts could overwhelm any opposition, even if of superior quality.

Early production D.Vs began reaching the front line in May 1917, with leading unit Jasta 11 amongst the early recipients. This squadron, led by Rittmeister Manfred von Richthofen, had claimed 89 victories for the loss of a single pilot during 'Bloody April'. It now began replacing its beloved D.IIIs with D.Vs, and the 'Red Baron' claimed his first success with the new type on 23 June. Early successes were tempered by the loss of several aircraft to structural failures whilst diving at or away from the enemy. And if that was not bad enough, German pilots were now encountering superior Allied types on a near-daily basis. One such aviator was Oberleutnant Ritter Adolf von Tutschek of Jasta 12:

'In the past four weeks three new types of enemy aircraft have appeared. They are without a doubt far superior in their ability to climb than the best D.V. They are the new English SE5 single-seater, the 200hp SPAD and the very outstanding Bristol Fighter two-seater. While the Albatros D.III and D.V come near in their ability to climb with the Sopwith and Nieuport, and even surpass them in speed, it is almost impossible for them to force an SE5 or a 200hp SPAD to fight because the enemy is able to avoid it by the ability of his craft.'

After describing the Bristol as 'our most dangerous opponent', von Tutschek got down to basics, speaking for virtually every German fighter pilot on the Western Front: 'In my opinion a machine superior to these three would be more important than an increase in the number of the present ones. I can achieve more with three pilots and aeroplanes that are completely trustworthy, as good or better than the opposition in climbing, manoeuvrability and sturdiness, than I can with 20 pilots in D.Vs of whose ability and performance I am not convinced, and must watch with apprehension while diving during air battle.'

Albatros attempted to rectify this situation by producing the D.Va in the autumn of 1917. However, this aircraft was little more than a strengthened D.V, powered by the same Mercedes D.III engine. And being heavier than both the D.V and the D.III, it was also slower – hardly what front-line fighter pilots wanted!

## ACES

Nearly every one of Germany's 81 Jagdstaffeln (fighter squadrons) operated one or more types of Albatros scout during World War One. This in turn meant that most of Idflieg's leading aces achieved victories with the aircraft. Easily the most famous ace to see action in a D.V/Va was Rittmeister Manfred Freiherr von Richthofen, who claimed his first victory with the aircraft (his 54th in total) on 23 June 1917 and his eighth on 30 November 1917. Other high-scoring pilots to make claims with the Albatros were Ernst Udet, Max Müller, Karl-Emil Schäfer and Julius Buckler.

Famed Bavarian ace Eduard Ritter von Schleich poses with the equally famous Albatros D.V that he flew as commander of Jasta 21. Von Schleich survived the war with 35 victories to his name.
*via Aviation-images.com*

continue to fight on in quantity, especially in the less active areas and with low-priority units.

More than 150 D.Vas were still serving as fighters when the Armistice came into effect on 11 November 1918, although none of these machines were being flown by elite Jagdgeschwader pilots. Despite lacking the profile of Fokker's legendary DrI or the impressive performance of its D.VII, the Albatros fighters' impact on aerial conflict in 1917-18 had been a significant one.

Albatros D.V D.1117/17 of Ltn d R Johann Janzen of Jasta 23, upended in the summer of 1917. The swastika on the fuselage was simply the unit marking of Jasta 23 at this time, the emblem having no political significance in World War One.
*via Aviation-images.com*

## KNIGHTS OF THE AIR

### Otto Könnecke

Born in Strasbourg on 20 September 1892, Könnecke began pilot training in 1913 at Flieger Erstaz Abteilung 4 in Metz. He subsequently served as a flying instructor from the outbreak of war in July 1914 through to 3 December 1916, when he was shipped off to Albatros-equipped Jasta 25 in Macedonia. After scoring an unconfirmed victory on 9 January 1917, Könnecke was credited with downing Serbian Farmans on 5 and 6 February, convincing his superiors to transfer him to the Western Front.

Vizefeldwebel Otto Könnecke claimed a number of victories with the Albatros D.V/Va during 1917-18. His tally had reached 35 by war's end.
*via Aviation-images.com*

From Armee Flugpark 2, he was assigned to Jasta 5 in April 1917. Vizefeldwebel Könnecke soon became one of the unit's so-called 'Golden Triumvirate', alongside fellow high-scoring Albatros aces Josef Mai and Fritz Rumey. Between them, these three pilots would be credited with shooting down 109 enemy aircraft – a significant number while at the controls of Albatros D.V/Vas.

Könnecke's Jasta 5 re-equipped with Fokker D.VIIs in May 1918, and on the 12 May he was awarded the Golden Military Merit Cross. On 15 June he was commissioned as a Leutnant, and on 20 July Könnecke received the Knight's Cross with Swords of the Royal Hohenzollern House Order. Finally, on 26 September, with his score at 32, he was awarded the coveted Orden Pour le Mérite. An SE5a on 18 October and DH4s on 1 and 4 November completed his tally at 35.

Post-war, Könnecke served as a pilot for Deutsche Luft Hansa from the airline's inception in 1926, and after joining the Luftwaffe in 1935 he rose to the rank of Major, commanding various flying schools. Following World War Two, Könnecke remained in Germany until his death on 25 January 1956.

Eagerly-anticipated replacements in the form of the Fokker DrI and Pfalz D.III would enter service in late 1917, but neither type would be produced in sufficient quantities to replace the by now obsolescent Albatros D.V/Va due to structural and mechanical failures (DrI) and poor performance (D.III).

During the massive German offensive of March and April 1918, most of the burden of aerial fighting fell on the shoulders of Albatros pilots – the elite Jagdgeschwader, however, were equipped with DrIs. Indeed, at the end of April 1918 there were no fewer than 928 D.Vas and 131 D.Vs on front-line strength, compared to 433 Pfalz D.IIIas and just 171 DrIs. This proved to be zenith of the D.Va's deployment in World War One, as from May onwards the outstanding Fokker D.VII began to appear in growing numbers. Nevertheless, the D.Va would

The scene at the site of the crash landing that put an end to Ltn d R Ernst Udet's Albatros D.Va in 1918.
*via Aviation-images.com*

# SURVIVORS

The subject of one of the finest restorations of any surviving World War One aircraft, D.Va D.7161/17 of the National Air and Space Museum (NASM) in Washington, DC.
*NASM*

JUST TWO COMPLETE examples of the Albatros D.V survive in museums today. The oldest of these is D.Va D.5390/17, which forms part of the 'Over the Front' exhibition in the Australian War Memorial's ANZAC Hall in Canberra. Built in August 1917 and issued to Jasta 29, the fighter was hit in the fuel tank whilst engaging an RE8 of No 69 (Australian) Squadron between Armentiéres and Ploegsteert Wood on the afternoon of 17 December 1917. Its pilot, Leutnant Rudolf Clauss, who had also suffered a thigh wound, hastily landed the

aircraft in Allied lines and was captured by troops of the 2nd Australian Division. The D.Va was retrieved by No 69 Squadron that night and trucked to its airfield at Bailleul. This was the first intact example of Albatros' latest fighter to fall into Allied hands, and it was shipped back to England and test-flown.

In 1919 the aircraft was sent to Australia. It was moved to Canberra's Aeroplane Hall in 1941, where the scout remained until 1966 when it was transferred to the Camden Museum of Aviation. The aircraft was restored and conserved in 2007-08 prior to being put on display as part of the 'Over the Front' exhibition in 2008.

The subject of one of the finest restorations of any surviving World War One aircraft, the second surviving D.Va is D.7161/17 (pictured above) of the National Air and Space Museum (NASM) in Washington, DC. Its operational career ended shortly after 15 April 1918, when a bullet penetrated the fighter's emergency fuel tank and lodged in the engine's right magneto.

## REPLICAS

A small number of Albatros D.V replicas have also been constructed over the years. Undoubtedly the most authentic reproduction D.Va in the world today is the aircraft built by New Zealand-based The Vintage Aviator Ltd (TVAL), which flew for the first time in late 2009. Powered by a restored Mercedes DIIIa engine, the aircraft is marked up as D.Va D.5284/17 of Jasta 5's Vizefeldwebel Josef Mai. Claiming seven victories with this machine (and four in an earlier D.V) in 1917-18, Mai had achieved 30 kills by war's end.

# SOPWITH CAMEL

THE MOST FAMOUS British fighting scout of World War One, the Sopwith Camel was also the most successful design to see service with either side in respect to the number of victories claimed by its pilots – 1,294 aeroplanes and three airships destroyed. The Camel was the first purpose-built British fighter to boast two Vickers machine guns synchronised to fire through the propeller arc. The humped fairing covering the breeches of these weapons actually provided the inspiration for the fighter's unique sobriquet, which, like its predecessor the Pup, went from being an unofficial appellation to its official name. Although the Camel boasted a fearsome reputation in combat, the fighter's exacting handling characteristics took a heavy toll on poorly trained novice pilots. Nevertheless, near on 5,500 Camels were eventually built.

**The Sopwith Camel scored more victories than any other aircraft during World War One.**
*Luigino Caliaro*

natural outgrowth of Sopwith's Pup and Triplane of 1916, the hump-backed Camel quickly had an impact on air warfare over the Western Front upon its introduction to front-line service in early June 1917. However, its formidable performance in combat came at a cost, for the aeroplane lost the peerless handling qualities of its predecessors. Once pilots gained familiarity with the Camel, they could make full use of its outstanding manoeuvrability and unmatched weight of fire, but in the beginning its unforgiving nature came as a nasty shock to aviators coming off docile training types or service machines like the Pup.

Sensitivity, skill and experience were needed to master the Camel, which had a tendency to drop its nose during a steep turn to starboard (the direction in which its large, weighty rotary engine was spinning). It also rose alarmingly with a port climbing turn (against the direction of the rotary engine, which spun around with the propeller). In both cases the pilot had to apply liberal amounts of left rudder to retain control of the scout.

Once these traits were mastered, the Camel proved to be one of the very best dogfighters of World War One. Indeed, the mass of its spinning engine allowed a skilled pilot to perform an unbelievably quick right-hand turn, which was accelerated by the torque of the rotary. In fact its rate of turn to the right was so pronounced that many pilots wishing to turn left chose to turn 270 degrees to starboard!

The inspiration behind the Camel came from the introduction of the Albatros D.I and D.II with twin synchronised machine guns to front-line Jastas in late 1916. The first examples of Sopwith's Pup and Triplane had only reached units in France in the autumn of that year, and although they were more than a match for the new German scouts, both fighters were only armed with a single synchronised Vickers 0.303in machine gun apiece.

A faster, more heavily armed aeroplane was urgently needed, so company owner T. O. M. Sopwith instructed his chief designer, Herbert Smith, to create an airframe that should not diverge too much from the Pup, yet be able to accommodate a larger, more powerful rotary engine and two machine guns. By following these principles, mass production of the new scout could be achieved in a short space of time following service approval.

During the autumn of 1916, while Pups and Triplanes struggled to cope with the Albatros menace, the Camel prototype (known as the F1) came together through the efforts of Smith and his small team. Designed specifically to house two Vickers 0.303in machine guns up-front, firing through the propeller, the scout bore more than a passing resemblance to the Pup. However, the design team had to have the main mass weight positioned right up front, with the engine, guns/ammunition, pilot, fuel

**Although tricky to fly, in the right hands the Sopwith Camel was a formidable dogfighter.**
*Luigino Caliaro*

**Garishly marked with an oriental-style dragon and a snake-eating bird on its fuselage, this unarmed F1 Camel was used by a training unit in England in 1918.**
*via Aviation-images.com*

and oil tanks all housed within the first third of the fuselage. Unlike the Pup, this gave the F1 prototype a squat and bullish appearance, the latter being a portent of what was to come from the machine both in respect to its handling qualities and ferociousness in combat once it reached the front line.

**ALTHOUGH HEAVILY** influenced by both the Pup and the Triplane, the Camel's genesis harked back to the Sopwith Tabloid racer of pre-war 1914. A boxy-looking, compact, single-bay biplane of wood and canvas, the machine's wing cellule was held together by cross-braced wire cables – a basic formula that would characterise most Sopwith designs for the rest of the war, including the Camel.

## 'THE CAMEL IS FIERCE, RAZOR-SHARP' Lt Arthur Gould Lee

The company's first proper fighting machine was the uniquely named 1 1/2 Strutter, which was co-designed by Herbert Smith. A two-seat reconnaissance-fighter and bomber, it featured a single 0.303in machine gun fitted with Sopwith-Kauper interruptor gear firing forward and a Scarff ring-mounted Lewis gun aft. The aircraft was named for its W-shaped cabane struts. By the time the 1 1/2 Strutter reached front-line service in early 1916, Sopwith had also created a single-seat scout based on the 'Hawker Runabout', designed in the autumn of 1915 by test pilot Harry Hawker.

Officially called the Scout, this machine impressed all who flew it thanks to its 110mph top speed, rate of climb, sprightly manoeuvrability and ease of handling. Powered by an 80hp Le Rhône rotary engine, this aircraft was ordered by both the RNAS and the RFC in April 1916. RFC officer Col Sefton Brancker was credited with the giving the aeroplane its popular name after declaring, 'Good God! Your 1 1/2 Strutter has had a pup' upon spotting a Scout alongside its two-seat forebear.

By the time the first Pups reached the RNAS' No 1 Wing at Dunkerque in July 1916, the prototype Sopwith Triplane was already on the continent undergoing combat evaluation. The fighter combined a Pup fuselage with three narrow-chord, high aspect ratio wings to give the pilot a better view from the cockpit, a faster rate of climb and superior manoeuvrability when compared with the Pup.

However, for all their virtues, both Sopwith fighters had a weakness in the slow rate of fire of their single Vickers guns when fitted with the Sopwith-Kauper interruptor gear. This became a real problem with the introduction of the Albatros D.I and D.II, whose twin synchronised machine guns gave them nearly triple the Sopwiths' rate of fire.

In December 1916, in response to this threat, the twin-gun F1 prototype, designed by Sopwith, R. J. Ashfield, Herbert Smith, F. Sigrist and Harry Hawker, was completed and flown for the first time on the 22nd of that month. The new aeroplane had a shorter, deeper fuselage than the Pup, with the engine, cockpit and guns concentrated within the foremost 7ft of its fuselage. In an effort to speed up production Sopwith eliminated the dihedral on the one-piece upper wing and compensated for its loss by doubling the dihedral of the lower wings to five degrees.

The prototype was powered by a 110hp Clerget 9Z rotary engine, and, as Harry Hawker put it, the aeroplane 'bounced into the air' from Brooklands aerodrome when he took it aloft for the first time. A highly experienced pilot, Hawker quickly noted that the torque of the spinning rotary engine, combined with the concentration of weight up front, gave the fighter outstanding manoeuvrability. Sensitivity was required when flying the scout, as was a judicious hand, especially during take-off.

Several other rotary engines of varying horsepower were trialled over the next few months in two subsequent prototypes that followed. When one of the these (F1/3) machines was delivered to the RFC's Testing Squadron at Martlesham Heath for service evaluation in March 1917, one of the unit's pilots commented, 'Just to look at the beast gives me the hump at the thought of flying it'. That remark, recorded by RFC technical officer Sir Henry Tizard, along with the appearance of the fairing that sloped up from the nose to partially cover the twin machine guns, led to the scout being unofficially christened the Camel.

By late May 1917 another prototype had been test-flown at Martlesham Heath with the new 150hp AR 1 rotary engine. A far more reliable unit than the Clerget thanks to its steel-lined aluminium cylinders, the engine, designed by RNAS engineering officer Wilfred Owen Bentley, was put into production as the Bentley BR1.

---

## CAMEL AT SEA

Like both the Pup and Triplane before it, the Camel was to be ordered by the RNAS as well as the RFC, but, unlike its forebears, the aeroplane was specially modified for naval use. A twin-float seaplane failed to gain much support from the Admiralty, though the 2F1 variant proved popular. The scout featured shorter-span wings, a narrower track undercarriage, a hinged, folding tail, and a single Vickers gun, supplemented by a 0.303in Lewis gun above the upper wing. Operating from warships and towed lighters, the 129 2F1s that were built enjoyed a successful career.

Also receiving a large number of conventional F1s, the RNAS gave the Camel its combat debut on the evening of 5 June 1917 when No 4 Naval Squadron pilot, and future ace, Alexander 'MacD' Shook claimed an Albatros D.III destroyed near Ostend. No 70 Squadron was the first RFC unit to take the aircraft into action when, on 27 June, Capt Clive F. Collett (also a future ace) downed an Albatros D.V. The creation of the Camel legend had commenced.

*Left:* **A Sopwith Camel takes off from the seaplane carrier HMS** *Pegasus*, **in the Firth of Forth in 1918.** *via Aviation-images.com*

*Bottom:* **This navalised 2F1 Camel is fitted with a single synchronised 0.303-in Vickers machine gun – standard armament for the RNAS Camel. The pilot standing before it is Maj Graham Donald.** *via Aviation-images.com*

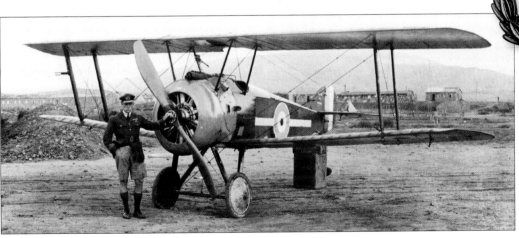

# FACT FILE

## CONSTRUCTION

### COCKPIT

The Camel had an open cockpit that left the occupant at the mercy of the elements. The fighter's famous gun fairing forward of the cockpit was created by Sopwith to protect the pilot from the worst of the slipstream, and the lubricants expelled by the spinning rotary engine. It proved ineffective, however, and a conventional windscreen was duly fitted. Like most fighters of 1917-18, the Camel's cockpit had three principal instruments – a tachometer, an altimeter and an airspeed indicator. Sat on a basket-work seat, the pilot had a tubular steel spade grip and a rudder control bar. The triggers for the guns were mounted in the centre of the spade grip.

### FUSELAGE

The Camel featured a box girder fuselage made up from ash longerons and spruce spacers, the whole structure being wire-braced, fabric-covered and surmounted by curved decking formed by stringers. The Camel's fin and rudder were strongly influenced by the Pup. Again, steel tube was employed in their construction, the fixed fin, rudder, tailplane and elevators being covered in fabric.

### WINGS

The wing structure was built up on twin spars of spindled spruce with spruce ribs and ash riblets. Steel tube was employed in the wingtips, while relatively small ailerons were fitted on the upper and lower wings. As originally designed, the Camel was to have featured about two-and-a-half degrees of dihedral on both upper and lower wings, but for ease of manufacture Sopwith decided to make the top wing flat. The dihedral of the lower wings was doubled to five degrees to compensate, thereby creating the Camel's distinctive 'pinched wing' appearance when viewed head-on.

### ARMAMENT

The Camel was the first Sopwith design to feature two 0.303in Vickers machine guns. Synchronised to fire through the propeller. The aircraft carried 500 rounds of ammunition in boxes below the weapons forward of the cockpit. The machine gun butts protruded into the cockpit at near eye level, and the pilot aimed these weapons using either Aldis ring-and-bead or tube gunsights. All Camel variants could carry four 20lb bombs in racks under the fuselage.

### ENGINE

Rotaries of French origin would power the majority of Camels, with Clerget 9B 130hp and Le Rhône 110hp engines initially dominating. From May 1917 the 150hp AR 1 rotary engine, designed by RNAS engineering liaison officer Wilfred Owen Bentley, was put into production as the Bentley BR1. Early Camels were blighted by engine maladies, with seizures or partial seizures caused by oil pump failure. Steel-lined aluminium cylinders made the BR1 a more reliable engine than its Clerget equivalent, making it very popular on the front line.

| 1916 | 1917 | | | |
|---|---|---|---|---|
| **22 December:** Sopwith F1 prototype takes to the air for the first time. | **4 May:** RNAS takes delivery of first Camels. | **5 June:** 4 Naval Squadron gives the Camel its combat debut. | **17 June:** No 70 Squadro becomes the fi RFC unit to re the Camel. |

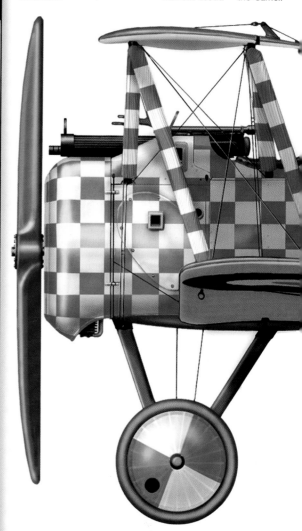

Camel D8239 of Capt C. M. McEwen, No 28 Squadron, Sarcedo, Italy, late 1918. *Courtesy Osprey Publishing*

## SPECIFICATIONS

### Sopwith F1 Camel

| | |
|---|---|
| **Engine:** | Clerget 9B |
| **Power:** | 130hp |
| **Max speed:** | 113mph (182km/h) |
| **Length:** | 18ft 9in (5.72m) |
| **Wingspan:** | 28ft 0in (8.53m) |
| **Height:** | 8ft 6in(2.59m) |
| **Armament:** | Two 0.303in Vickers machine guns |
| **Max all-up weight:** | 1,453lb (659kg) |
| **Range:** | 250 miles (400km) |
| **Number built:** | 5,490 |
| **Entered service:** | May 1917 |

1918

| **4 September:** | **19 September:** | **1918** — **21 April:** | **30 May:** | **11 August:** | **24 September:** | **1920** — **31 October:** |
|---|---|---|---|---|---|---|
| No 44 Squadron scrambles two Camels to attack Gotha bombers attacking south-east England at night. | No 70 Squadron and No 10 Naval Squadron carry out the first organised ground attack missions by Camels, against trenches and troop positions along the Ypres front. | Canadian ace Capt Roy Brown of No 209 Squadron is officially credited with shooting down the 'Red Baron', Rittmeister Manfred Freiherr von Richthofen. | Col Charles Rumney Samson attempts to take off from a towed lighter in a skid-equipped 2F1 Camel off the coast of Orfordness. The aircraft falls over the side and is smashed to pieces. Samson is rescued unhurt. | Camel 2F1 pilot Lt Stuart C. Culley is credited with claiming the last German airship to be shot down in World War One, Zeppelin L53 crashing in Heligoland Bight. | The Camel-equipped 17th and 148th Aero Squadrons of the United States Air Service in France shoot down 11 German aircraft between them. | A total of 2,519 F1 and 129 2F1 Camels are on RAF charge. |

8239D

**IN CLOSE-UP**

The business end of a Camel, the first Sopwith design to feature two 0.303in Vickers machine guns, the butts for which protruded into the cockpit at near eye level.

*Luigino Caliaro*

## DID YOU KNOW?

- The Camel could trace its lineage to the Sopwith Tabloid, which was originally conceived in late 1913 as a two-seat sporting biplane whose layout was chalked up on the floor of a skating rink – then T. O. M. Sopwith's 'factory' in Kingston-upon-Thames.

- The Camel was built with fairings that sloped upward from the nose and covered the breeches of its twin machine guns. Pilots that saw early examples of the aeroplane thought that the fairings looked like humps, hence the fighter's 'Camel' nickname.

- Sopwith introduced cut-outs in the upper wing section to alleviate the pilot's restricted view upward and forward. A serious weakness in the Camel's design, pilots would cut even larger apertures in the upper wing in the field.

- The first front-line Camel loss came on 13 June 1917 when American volunteer pilot, and Pup ace, Sub-Lt Langley F. W. Smith, was killed 'stunting' in his aeroplane over the German aerodrome at Neumünster.

- Aside from seeing action as day fighters on the Western and Italian fronts, Camels also equipped Home Defence units in southern England. These machines flew night missions against German Gotha and AEG bombers sent to attack London.

- Two squadrons of the United States Air Service also saw considerable action with the Camel in France from the summer of 1918 through to war's end.

- Camel B6313, flown by Maj 'Billy' Barker, was credited with the destruction of no fewer than 46 enemy aircraft between 20 October 1917 and 18 September 1918. Canadian Barker survived the war with 50 victories to his name.

# FROM THE COCKPIT

THE CAMEL WAS a mercilessly unforgiving aeroplane, but for those who mastered it the Sopwith scout was a dogfighter of the first order. Indeed, the Camel's lack of stability and extreme sensitivity were assets in the hands of a competent pilot and potentially fatal to the novice. It had a turning capability unmatched by any other fighter bar the Fokker DrI, but if the turn was tightened too much the Camel would spin. This was usually the end result of coarse handling. The Camel was markedly tail-heavy at full throttle, making it tiring to fly. The pilot also suffered from poor upward vision, and by 1918 it lacked the speed and rate of climb of its more modern German opponents. However, it more than made up for these deficiencies with an instantaneous response to the slightest touch on the controls. Its manoeuvrability was outstanding thanks primarily to the concentration of all the principal weight masses – engine, guns, pilot and fuel – within a very small section of the fuselage.

Pup ace Lt Arthur Gould Lee of No 46 Squadron was a strong proponent of the Camel, flying the aircraft from November 1917 in the Cambrai offensive.

*'First impressions – more room in the cockpit than the Pup, so you can take a deep*

## CLAIRMARAIS CAMEL

Sopwith Camel number B7407 of No 54 Squadron on approach to Clairmarais aerodrome on 23 April 1918. On this day the machine was being flown by Lt Waring, but he crashed the Camel upon landing. Fortunately he walked away from the incident.
*Painting by Russell Smith*

breath without feeling you're going to burst the fuselage at the seams (but why on earth didn't they fit it with a parachute?) Second, the exciting pull of the 130hp Clerget, and the surge of power at full throttle. Third, her amazing lightness on the controls, lighter even than a Pup, which is gentle-sensitive, while the Camel is fierce, razor-sharp. She turns with lightning quickness to the right. You have to be careful taking off as the engine torque veers her to the left, and you have to apply full right rudder, but it's easy enough once you get the knack. I've not fired the guns yet, that's a pleasure to come.

'She loops practically automatically, as she is tail-heavy – so much so that in level flying you have to press against the joystick the whole time. Result, if you don't press, she just goes up and over. But you have to watch your rudder. She does a very fast flick-roll – on the Pup this calls for a certain knack, but the Camel goes round effortlessly and instantly.

'I found it tiring to fly in formation for a long patrol. She's so sensitive you can't relax for a second, and you have the constant pressure on the joystick, which in two hours' flying makes your right arm ache. But she's such a marvellous aeroplane that these handicaps are unimportant.'

Lee was a highly experienced aviator who had the experience to master the Camel. Many of the pilots on the Western Front at this time were relative novices, and the report from No 73 Squadron's A Flight on 19 October 1917 was perhaps more indicative of how the majority viewed the new Sopwith scout:

'Everyone was fit for flying, getting along okay, but not as keen as they should be. Seem to have the wind up about Camels.'

# IN COMBAT

**THE FIRST CAMELS** were delivered to the RNAS in May 1917 following an Admiralty order for 50 examples. These were issued to No 4 Naval Squadron at Bray Dunes, in France, early the following month, and the unit gave the Camel its combat debut on the evening of 5 June 1917 when Flight Commander Alexander 'MacD' Shook claimed an Albatros D.III destroyed near Ostend. By the end of July four RNAS units had swapped their Pups and Triplanes for Camels.

That same month No 70 Squadron became the first unit in the RFC to receive the new Sopwith scout, replacing its 1 1/2 Strutters at Liettres. The squadron had sufficient aeroplanes to support the Ypres offensive in late July. The following month Camels started to reach Home Defence units, starting with the 1 1/2 Strutter-equipped No 44 Squadron at Hainault Farm. Charged with defending London from night raiders, the unit began the challenging task of flying the Camel after dark.

The squadron's experience with the aircraft led directly to the development of a dedicated Camel night fighter, which had its Vickers gun removed (their muzzle flash obliterated the pilot's night vision) and a pair of Lewis guns fitted to a double Foster mounting on the upper wing section. The cockpit was also repositioned 12 inches further back to allow the pilot to aim and reload the guns. Finally, the fuel tanks were moved to the forward fuselage to compensate for the aft movement of the cockpit.

By late 1917 Camels were being flown operationally by nine RFC and six RNAS squadrons in France, two RFC squadrons in Italy and No 44 Squadron in Home Defence. Some 3,450 examples had been ordered, and the fighter was being built at nine factories in the UK.

Although performing very well in its designed role as a fighter, the Camel was also well-suited to ground attack operations too. Its cockpit was further forward than its great rival the SE5A, which gave the pilot a better view of the ground at low level, while its turning ability gave the Camel the edge if challenged by ground fire. The first real test for the aeroplane in this new role came during the Cambrai offensive of November 1917.

## ACES

Camel pilots were responsible for downing 1,294 enemy aircraft between June 1917 and November 1918, so it was inevitable that a large number of Allied pilots would 'make ace' flying the aeroplane. Indeed, no fewer than 19 pilots claimed 20 or more victories with the Sopwith scout, with the ranking aces on this list being Capt Donald MacLaren with 54 victories, Maj 'Billy' Barker with 46 and Maj John Gilmour with 36. At least two RFC pilots claimed six kills in a day with the Camel, and Canadian ace Capt Roy Brown was officially credited with shooting down the 'Red Baron', Rittmeister Manfred Freiherr von Richthofen.

The only Victoria Cross to be won by a Camel pilot was awarded to Lt Alan Jerrard of No 66 Squadron when his flight of three aircraft was jumped by 19 enemy fighters during an attack on an Austrian airfield. Jerrard fought the fighters alone, claiming two destroyed and allowing his squadron-mates to escape. His aircraft was badly shot up, and he was forced to land and be captured.

*Eight-victory ace 1st Lt Henry R. Clay of the 148th Aero Squadron prepares to haul himself aboard Camel 'E' of 'A' Flight at Petite Synthe in August 1918. Clay succumbed to influenza on 17 February 1919.*
*via Aviation-images.com*

*The 148th Aero Squadron was one of two United States Air Service squadrons to be equipped with Camels in France during the summer of 1918. Photographed at Petite Synthe, near Dunkirk, on 6 August 1918, the lead aircraft in this line-up (D9516) was shot down on 26 August and its pilot, 1st Lt George Vaughn Seibold, killed.*
*via Aviation-images.com*

At the forefront of operations was No 46 Squadron, which was briefed to support tanks (being used on a massive scale for the first time) by attacking ground targets, including gun positions, as well as bombing nearby German aerodromes. The unit flew ceaselessly in challenging weather conditions during the campaign, and there is no doubt that its aerial attacks inflicted significant casualties on German troops, and adversely affected their morale. Having seen how successful the Camel was in the ground attack role, the RFC and RAF would commit more fighter units to the mission for the remaining months of the war.

Pilots keen to engage the 'Hun' in aerial combat were not keen on ground attack missions, as Lt Arthur Gould Lee of No 46 Squadron recalled: *'Imagine, after waiting all those months for Camels, striving not to be shot down on Pups, and looking forward to toppling Huns two at a time with my Vickers, to find myself switched to ground strafing!'*

The air fighting in France during 1918 was some of the toughest of the entire war, and the Camel squadrons were in the vanguard of the action. Typical unit strength was increased early in the year from 18 to 24 aircraft, and, by the start of the final great German offensive of the conflict on 21 March, seven squadrons had achieved this planned establishment. These larger units enjoyed great success, with Nos 73 and 80 Squadrons claiming six German aircraft in a single patrol on 22 March, ace Capt J. L. Trollope of No 43 Squadron downing six machines 48 hours later and squadron-mate H. W. Woollett equalling this feat on 12 April.

In Italy, four Camel units (Nos 28, 66, 139 and 225 Squadrons) fought the Austro-Hungarians throughout 1918.

At sea, navalised 2F1 Camels operating with the Home Fleet attacked German airships and seaplanes over the North Sea. Flying from

## KNIGHTS OF THE AIR

### Donald MacLaren

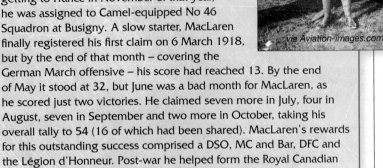

The leading Camel ace in terms of victories scored in the Sopwith fighter was Canadian Donald Roderick MacLaren. Born in Ottawa on 28 May 1893, he moved with his family to Calgary, and as a boy he became an expert marksman with a rifle. Poor health prevented an immediate entry into military service, but in May 1917 MacLaren joined the RFC and became a flight instructor in Ontario. Finally getting to France in November of that year, he was assigned to Camel-equipped No 46 Squadron at Busigny. A slow starter, MacLaren finally registered his first claim on 6 March 1918, but by the end of that month – covering the German March offensive – his score had reached 13. By the end of May it stood at 32, but June was a bad month for MacLaren, as he scored just two victories. He claimed seven more in July, four in August, seven in September and two more in October, taking his overall tally to 54 (16 of which had been shared). MacLaren's rewards for this outstanding success comprised a DSO, MC and Bar, DFC and the Légion d'Honneur. Post-war he helped form the Royal Canadian Air Force. He passed away in July 1989.

*via Aviation-images.com*

lighters towed behind destroyers as part of the Harwich Force, a 2F1 Camel was credited with claiming the last German airship to be shot down in World War One on 11 August 1918, Zeppelin L53 crashing in Heligoland Bight. Two others had been destroyed on 19 July when seven aircraft from HMS *Furious* attacked the airship sheds at Tondern with 50lb bombs. Only two Camels returned safely to *Furious*, however.

Although progressively replaced by the Sopwith Snipe in the final months of World War One, Camels remained in service with the RAF well into 1920.

**1st Lt George Wyly served with the 148th Aero Squadron in the final months of World War One. He survived the conflict with four victories to his name.**
*via Aviation-images.com*

# SURVIVORS

OF THE ALMOST 5,500 Sopwith F1 and 2F1 Camels that were built, just seven complete, genuine examples are known to have survived. The best known British-based example is F1 F6314, which has been resident in the RAF Museum at Hendon since its opening in 1972. Having been purchased privately in 1923 from the Aircraft Disposal Company, this war-surplus machine passed through several owners until it was acquired by the Royal Aeronautical Society in 1953. Moved to London Airport in 1960, the fighter was restored by British European Airways over the next three years and passed on permanent loan to the embryo RAF Museum. It has remained there ever since.

One of the most notable Camels in the UK is 2F1 N6812, which Lt Stuart C. Culley used to down Zeppelin L53 on 11 August 1918. The aircraft was then ditched alongside HMS *Redoubt*, which had been towing the lighter from which Culley had taken off. Both pilot and aircraft were soon retrieved. The Camel was handed over to the Imperial War Museum in the early 1920s, and after some years in storage the fighter was put on display at the IWM's Lambeth home in 1935. N6812 was damaged during an air raid on London in January 1941 and eventually restored and put back on display in 1953. More sympathetically overhauled by Skysport Engineering in the late 1980s, it remains a prized exhibit in the IWM's Lambeth museum today.

*via Aviation-images.com*

*Below:* **Embracing the spirit of an age, this immaculate Sopwith Camel replica (complete with rotary engine) is flown by Vintage Aviator Ltd in New Zealand.**
*Luigino Caliaro*

## REPLICAS

A significant number of replica Camels powered by a whole host of engines have been built over the years, with some of the more famous examples being Cole Palen's Old Rhinebeck collection aircraft and the two F1s built by Viv Bellamy of Leisure Sport, all three of which were powered by rotary engines of various origins.

# FOKKER TRIPLANE

**UNDOUBTEDLY THE MOST** famous fighter type to see service on either side during World War One, the Fokker DrI was inspired by the Sopwith Triplane of 1916-17. Boasting three superimposed wings, the British scout enjoyed much better manoeuvrability than any other fighter then in service over the Western Front. In response, the Fokker Flugzeugwerke devised the Dreidecker (hence 'Dr'), which completed its first flight in June 1917 and entered service two months later. Rittmeister Manfred Freiherr von Richthofen's Jagdgeschwader I, known as the 'Flying Circus', was the first unit to completely re-equip with the new fighter, and in the skilled hands of its numerous aces, the DrI proved a formidable opponent.

The feared sight of a Fokker DrI closing in for the kill, its pilot hunched behind its two deadly Spandau machine guns.
*Luigino Caliaro*

The iconic Fokker DrI owes its very existence to the success enjoyed by the less well-known Sopwith Triplane of 1916. The triplane concept of three superimposed wings was not a new design when the British scout entered front-line service with the RNAS in France in July 1916. However, its superior performance over its Fokker and Albatros rivals at the time came as an unpleasant surprise to the German authorities. Idflieg (Inspektion der Fliegertruppen – the Inspectorate of Military Aviation) immediately ordered all German aeroplane manufacturers to submit triplane fighter designs and 14 were quickly built.

Leading the pack was the Fokker Flugzeugwerke, which had been developing a series of prototype scouts that featured a pioneering box spar wing structure. The latter offered a lightweight airframe that made the most of the limited power that engines of the time produced. Testing of these machines had begun in early 1917 – months prior to the Idflieg issuing its triplane request. Keen to regain the prominent position he had once occupied as chief supplier of German fighting scouts thanks to his Fokker E series of 1915-16, company principal Anthony Fokker instructed his chief designer, Reinhold Platz, to modify one of the prototypes into a three-winged triplane.

Initially powered by a captured French 110hp Le Rhône air-cooled rotary engine, the first prototype made its maiden flight in early July 1917. The aircraft impressed Idflieg, and

**Flying circus – Jasta 11's wartime activities are commemorated in this amazing sight of seven Fokker triplane replicas in flight in New Zealand.** *Gavin Conroy*

Fokker was ordered to commit the design to production. Early flight trials had revealed that the prototype's stubby, deep, unbraced wings suffered from undesirable buffet, so Platz redesigned the wings with slightly shallower sections, greater span and balanced ailerons. Crucially, he also added interplane struts to make the flying surfaces less flexible. Powered by an Oberursel UrII – a German copy of the Le Rhône rotary – and armed with a pair of 7.92mm Maxim LMG 08/15 'Spandau' machine guns utilising interrupter gear to fire through the propeller, the definitive Fokker DrI triplane was born.

A trio of pre-production FIs was built in August and single examples supplied to leading aces Rittmeister Manfred Freiherr von Richthofen and Leutnant Werner Voss. Their exploits with these aircraft in the autumn of 1917 quickly created a myth of invincibility surrounding the Fokker triplane that preceded the DrI's introduction to service in October of that year.

Just 320 triplanes would be built, yet the fighter has come to symbolise the exploits of World War One's 'Knights of the Air' more than any other aircraft from this period.

## WHEN RITTMEISTER Manfred

Freiherr von Richthofen first encountered a Sopwith Triplane in April 1917, he wrote that *'the Sopwith Triplane is the best aircraft the enemy possesses. It climbs better, is more manoeuvrable and does not lose altitude in*

*a bank, is faster and can be dived straight down'.* However, this did not prevent him from shooting it down! But because of the views of Germany's leading ace, and general grumblings of discontent coming from other veteran fighter pilots of the time about their aircraft, the Idflieg hastily called for the creation of a German triplane to rival the British scout. Fokker would ultimately secure the contract to build the new fighter.

Anthony Fokker had an advantage over rival designers when it came to producing the triplane, as he had been briefed on the Sopwith fighter's outstanding performance by none other than Rittmeister Manfred Freiherr von Richthofen himself during a visit he made to Jasta 11 shortly after the 'Red Baron's' encounter with the RNAS machine. Von Richthofen urged Fokker to build such an aeroplane, and the Dutchman was also taken to a forward observation post to see the British fighter in action. He also inspected a captured example at Adlershof a short while later.

Yet despite his intimate knowledge of the Sopwith scout, Fokker furnished his chief designer Reinhold Platz with only the barest details about the British machine. This in turn meant that the aircraft was an entirely new design, and not just a copy of the Triplane. Fokker made the decision to produce a Dreidecker on 15 June 1917, instructing Platz to modify the V4 scout prototype that he was then working on for the Austro-Hungarian government into a triplane. He gave his chief designer a briefing on the Sopwith scout's basic layout, but left the technical details to Platz.

What he came up with used a cantilevered box spar wing structure as had been trialled on Fokker's previous V1 through V3 sesquiplane prototypes. Their strength was based upon the use of a composite box spar that was built up by joining two subsidiary box spars through the employment of plywood webs. The lower wing, which had the same chord as the middle wing but was of slightly reduced span, was clamped to the lower fuselage longeron tubes. Of the three wings, only the top one, of greater span than the other two and set above the fuselage on a pair of inverted vee struts, had unbalanced ailerons.

An accomplished pilot who had taught himself to fly, Fokker took the V4 aloft for the first time on 5 July 1917 and commented upon his return that the aircraft's light construction gave it a good power-to-weight ratio. This in turn made it highly aerobatic. Idflieg officials and visiting Service pilots flew the aircraft in coming weeks, and on 14 July Fokker received an order for 20 aeroplanes. Three of these would be completed as FI pre-production machines (designated V5s by Fokker), and they differed from the V4 in having a greater wingspan, balanced ailerons and elevators, a reshaped tailplane and, perhaps most importantly of all, thin interplane struts.

The FI metamorphosed into the production DrI after thorough testing by Idflieg at Adlershof

in the late summer of 1917, Fokker receiving an order for 100 examples in September. Of the three FIs built, one was tested to destruction and the remaining two saw brief action with Jastas 10 and 11 before being shot down. The experience gained with these aircraft in the front line led to wooden skids being added beneath the lower wingtips, as the FIs had proven difficult to manoeuvre under power on the ground. Aileron area was also increased on production aircraft.

The first DrI was delivered to Jasta 15 on 11 October. By month end a series of accidents had grounded the aircraft, and a close inspection of the surviving machines revealed both bad workmanship and the use of sub-standard materials in the construction of the wings. Rectification work was swiftly carried out, with wings being built to an improved standard. It took a full month for the flying ban to be removed from the DrI, however, and by 1 December only 31 aircraft had been delivered, rather than the planned 173.

## 'IT CLIMBED LIKE A MONKEY AND WAS AS MANOEUVRABLE AS THE DEVIL' Rittmeister Manfred Freiherr von Richthofen

Despite remaining the most agile fighter on the Western Front, and being able to hold its own until the late spring of 1918, the DrI was hamstrung by the performance of its Oberursel rotary engine, which produced just 110hp and gave the fighter a top speed of 112mph. Its rivals were up to 20mph faster. The aircraft could not dive under full power either because of its questionable construction and the drag caused by its thick wings. Nevertheless, the DrI was a much feared opponent in the skies over France and Belgium from late 1917 through to the summer of 1918, when it was no longer a match for the SE5as, Camel F1s and SPAD VIIs and XIIIs being issued in large numbers to Allied fighter units.

# FROM THE COCKPIT

THE DRI WAS not an easy aeroplane to fly, as its inherent instability meant that the pilot had to remain vigilant at all times when in the air. Thanks to its short wingspan and the lift offered by its three wings and axle fairing, the fighter was supremely manoeuvrable. Indeed, those British pilots that survived an encounter with the aircraft over the Western Front commented on this over and over again.

One such individual was high-scoring SE5a ace Capt James McCudden of No 56 Squadron, who fought Ltn Werner Voss in the epic clash of 23 September 1917: *'By now the triplane was in the middle of our formation and its handling was wonderful to behold. The pilot seemed to be firing at all of us simultaneously, and although I got behind him a second time I could hardly stay there for a second. His movements were so quick and uncertain that none of us could hold him in our sight at all for any decisive time.'*

Fellow No 56 Squadron ace Capt Geoffrey Bowman was also involved in this engagement with Voss, and he remarked afterwards: *'I put my nose down to give him a burst and opened fire, perhaps too soon. To my amazement he kicked on full rudder, without bank, pulled his nose up slightly, gave me a burst while he was skidding sideways and then kicked on opposite rudder before the results of this amazing stunt appeared to have any effect on the controllability of his machine.'*

However, the odds were stacked too high against Voss and after a valiant fight, he was eventually shot down and killed by the circling pack of SE5s.

German 11-victory ace Ltn Rudolf Stark briefly flew hand-me-down DrIs with Royal Bavarian Jagdstaffel 34 in May 1918. Following his first flight in the aircraft he wrote: *'Flying these new machines is at first naturally very unfamiliar. Light and sensitive, they follow the slightest movement of the controls. They climb like a lift, and in the twinkling of an eye are several hundred metres high. One can turn on a spot like a top. The operation of the rotary engine has to be learned first though, and in the beginning created some difficulties.'*

Just as the triplane was a handful in the air, the DrI also demanded the respect of its pilot when on the ground, as visibility forward from the cockpit was restricted by the wings and large engine cowling. This was also the case once aloft, with pilots commenting that they had to move the triplane around to see obscured areas of sky ahead of them. Thanks to its light weight, the aircraft boasted good acceleration and a short take-off run. Lacking a fin, the fighter was unstable in yaw. The gyroscopic action of the rotary engine made turning right in the aircraft easier than turning left.

## The 'Red Baron'

THE MOST SUCCESSFUL pilot of World War One, Manfred Freiherr von Richthofen will always be inextricably linked with the Fokker DrI. He was born on 2 May 1892 in the Lower Silesian town of Kleinberg, near Schweidnitz. His father was a retired career Army officer, and Manfred was destined to follow in his footsteps – he entered the Cadet Institute at Wahlstatt at the age of 11. He graduated to the Main Cadet Institute at Gross-Lichterfelde in 1909, and was commissioned as a leutnant in the Silesian Ulanen-Regiment (Kaiser Alexander III von Russland) Nr 1 in 1912. When the war began von Richthofen's unit was sent to the eastern front, and he saw service both in Russia and France. Dissatisfied with the inaction he experienced on the latter front, he petitioned to transfer to the air service, which he did in May 1915.

After training as an observer, von Richthofen was sent back to the eastern front with Feldflieger Abteilung 69, and then served with Brieftauben Abteilung Ostende – a cover name for a multi-task unit which operated over the Flanders

Front. After a chance meeting with leading ace Oswald Boelcke, he was inspired to pursue pilot training, and completed this in December 1915. While serving as a pilot with Kampfgeschwader 2 in Russia, von Richthofen was recruited for Boelcke's new Jasta 2. Flying the Albatros D.II, he rewarded Boelcke's faith in him by downing an FE2B on 17 September 1916 – the momentous first of an eventual 80 victories. After Boelcke's death on 28 October, von Richthofen really showed his promise when he downed the DH2 of Maj Lanoe G. Hawker, Britain's premier fighter tactician, on 23 November for his 11th victory.

On 10 January 1917 von Richthofen was made commander of Jasta 11, and two days later he received news that he was to receive the coveted Pour le Mérite, which followed his 24th claim. As a Staffelführer, he proved to be as skilful a leader, trainer and organiser as he was a fighter pilot. Von Richthofen was promoted to the rank of Rittmeister on 6 April. By the end of 'Bloody April' von Richthofen had surpassed his idol Boelcke's score with 53 victories, and his Jasta 11 was famous throughout Germany. It was only logical that he be given command of the first Fighter Wing in the Luftstreitkräfte,

but his leadership of Jagdgeschwader I was soon interrupted by a near-fatal head wound on 6 July.

Von Richthofen returned to combat far too soon, and he was plagued by headaches and exhaustion after every flight. Nonetheless, his was a war of duty, and he persevered. Although many of his superiors and his family urged him to retire from combat flying, he refused. In March and April 1918, von Richthofen seemed at last to be back to his old form, scoring 16 kills in less than six weeks. His death on 21 April remains the subject of controversy, with both Camel ace Capt Roy Brown of No 209 Squadron and Australian troops on the ground claiming to have fired the fatal shot that hit him in the head as his DrI crested Morlancourt Ridge. What cannot be disputed is that von Richthofen's tally of 80 victories would remain unsurpassed by war's end.

Buried with full military honours at Bertangles, Rittmeister Manfred Freiherr von Richthofen's remains have been moved several times since then, and his grave is now in Wiesbaden, Germany

**'Bringing the Guns to Bear'** is a depiction of the final SE5 victory of Manfred von Richthofen. The victim was Lt J. P. McCone of No 41 Squadron.
*Painting by Russell Smith*

# FACT FILE

# CONSTRUCTION

### COCKPIT

The pilot of the DrI was sat in an open and somewhat snug cockpit exposed to the elements. The cockpit boasted just three instruments, namely an airspeed indicator, compass and altimeter, whilst nestled between the 'Spandau' guns at eye level was the fuel gauge.

### FUSELAGE

Of rectangular cross-section, the fuselage was made up of thin-walled mild-steel tubes. These were internally rigged with single strands of piano wire to give it structural strength. Fabric rather than plywood was used to cover the fuselage, as this was lighter. The fuselage top decking in front of the cockpit was made up of a series of shaped aluminium sheets, as were the cockpit sides.

### TAIL

The DrI had no fin, instead relying on its flat fuselage sides for lateral stability. The comma-shaped one-piece rudder, the roughly triangular tailplane and the one-piece elevators were made of welded steel tubing covered in fabric.

### WINGS

The DrI's most distinctive feature was its three wings, which were strong cantilever structures that were strong enough to withstand punishing combat manoeuvring. The wings' strength came from its use of a composite box spar that was built up by joining two subsidiary box spars through the employment of plywood webs.

### ARMAMENT

The DrI was armed with two LMG 08/15 'Spandau' machine guns, synchronised using Fokker's Zentralsteurung interruptor gear. The aircraft carried 1,000 rounds of ammunition in boxes below the weapons forward of the cockpit. The machine gun butts protruded into the cockpit at near eye level, and the pilot aimed these weapons using a ring-and-bead sight at the very end of the weapons.

### UNDERCARRIAGE

The fixed undercarriage was of conventional design for the period, consisting of streamline section steel-tube vee struts. The axle was encased in a mixed construction 'sub-wing' that provided the DrI with significant additional lift in flight.

### ENGINE

The principal DrI engine was the Oberursel Ur II, a copy of the French 110hp Le Rhône. For all the efforts put into it, the DrI never acquired an engine of true reliability, which handicapped its effectiveness during the spring of 1918 and practically drove it from the skies as the warm summer weather taxed its synthetic lubricants beyond their limits.

## SPECIFICATIONS

### Fokker DrI

| | |
|---|---|
| **Engine:** | Oberursel Ur II |
| **Power:** | 110hp |
| **Max speed:** | 103mph (165km/h) |
| **Length:** | 18ft 11in (5.77m) |
| **Wing span:** | 23ft 7in (7.19m) |
| **Height:** | 9ft 8in (3.48m) |
| **Armament:** | Two 7.92mm Maxim LMG 08/15 'Spandau' machine guns |
| **Max all-up weight:** | 1,289lb (586kg) |
| **Range:** | 130 miles (208kg) |
| **Number built:** | 320 |
| **Entered service:** | October 1917 |

## 1917

**28 August:**
Fls 102/17 and 103/17 delivered to Jagdgeschwader I and allotted to Rittmeister Manfred Freiherr von Richthofen and to Ltn Werner Voss of Jasta 10.

**1 September:**
Rittmeister Manfred Freiherr von Richthofen, flying Fl 102/17, scores first Fokker triplane victory – over an RE8.

**3 September:**
Rittmeister Manfred Freiherr von Richthofen brings down a Sopwith Pup while Leutnant Werner Voss, flying Fl 103/17, destroys a Camel.

**11 October**
First DrI delivered to JG I's Jasta 15

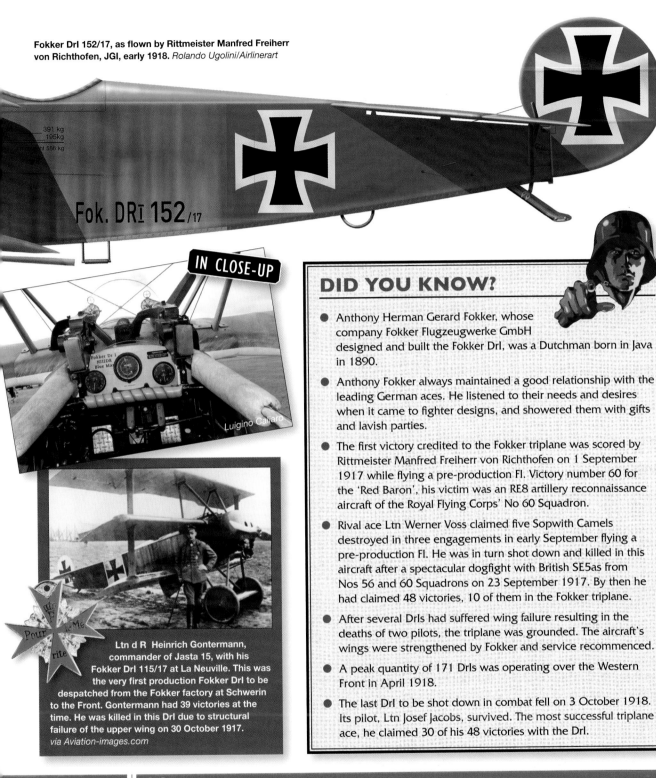

Fokker DrI 152/17, as flown by Rittmeister Manfred Freiherr von Richthofen, JGI, early 1918. *Rolando Ugolini/Airlinerart*

391 kg
195kg
586 kg

Fok. DRI 152/17

IN CLOSE-UP

*Luigino Callaro*

Ltn d R Heinrich Gontermann, commander of Jasta 15, with his Fokker DrI 115/17 at La Neuville. This was the very first production Fokker DrI to be despatched from the Fokker factory at Schwerin to the Front. Gontermann had 39 victories at the time. He was killed in this DrI due to structural failure of the upper wing on 30 October 1917. *via Aviation-images.com*

## DID YOU KNOW?

- Anthony Herman Gerard Fokker, whose company Fokker Flugzeugwerke GmbH designed and built the Fokker DrI, was a Dutchman born in Java in 1890.

- Anthony Fokker always maintained a good relationship with the leading German aces. He listened to their needs and desires when it came to fighter designs, and showered them with gifts and lavish parties.

- The first victory credited to the Fokker triplane was scored by Rittmeister Manfred Freiherr von Richthofen on 1 September 1917 while flying a pre-production FI. Victory number 60 for the 'Red Baron', his victim was an RE8 artillery reconnaissance aircraft of the Royal Flying Corps' No 60 Squadron.

- Rival ace Ltn Werner Voss claimed five Sopwith Camels destroyed in three engagements in early September flying a pre-production FI. He was in turn shot down and killed in this aircraft after a spectacular dogfight with British SE5as from Nos 56 and 60 Squadrons on 23 September 1917. By then he had claimed 48 victories, 10 of them in the Fokker triplane.

- After several DrIs had suffered wing failure resulting in the deaths of two pilots, the triplane was grounded. The aircraft's wings were strengthened by Fokker and service recommenced.

- A peak quantity of 171 DrIs was operating over the Western Front in April 1918.

- The last DrI to be shot down in combat fell on 3 October 1918. Its pilot, Ltn Josef Jacobs, survived. The most successful triplane ace, he claimed 30 of his 48 victories with the DrI.

### 1918

| November: | December: | 13 January: | 21 March: | 20 April: | 21 April: | 18 May: | June-July: | 3 October: |
|---|---|---|---|---|---|---|---|---|
| After several ases of wing ailure, Idflieg rounds all DrIs pending investigation. | Deliveries of DrIs with improved construction procedures resume. | Ltn Eberhardt Stapenhorst is brought down by ground fire and his DrI, 144/17, falls into British hands intact. | DrIs, equipping elements of JGs I, II and III, are the best German fighters available as the 'Kaiserschlacht', Germany's last great offensive of World War One, commences. | Rittmeister Manfred Freiherr von Richthofen downs two Camels, bringing his total to 80. | Rittmeister Manfred Freiherr von Richthofen is killed – probably by ground fire – while fighting with Camels. | First Fokker D.VIIs arrive at Jasta 11, which begins the process of passing its DrIs to other units. | Rotary engine seizures, mainly due to the failure of castor oil substitute lubricant in the summer heat, ground an entire Staffel of DrIs as D.VIIs replace them. | The last DrI to be shot down in combat falls during an attack on Jasta 7's St Marguerite airfield. Its pilot, Ltn Josef Jacobs, survives. |

# IN COMBAT

THE FOKKER TRIPLANE had an immediate impact on aerial combat over the Western Front, as the two pre-production FIs issued to Jastas 10 and 11 for front-line evaluation were quickly thrown into action. Indeed, Rittmeister Manfred Freiherr von Richthofen made his first flight in the aircraft on 1 September 1917 and scored his first victory with the aircraft later that same day. Leutnant Werner Voss used the second FI to make his first claim with the triplane two days later. Both aircraft had been lost by 23 September, however, with Voss falling on this date and the other FI having been shot down by RNAS Camels eight days earlier while being flown by ace Oberleutnant Kurt Wolff.

The first production DrIs reached JG I in October 1917, and it was intended that enough aircraft would be built to

## ACES

A number of high-scoring German aces flew the DrI in combat, with the leading exponent being Josef Jacobs who claimed more than 30 of his 44-48 victories with the aircraft. Others to score a significant number of kills were Manfred von Richthofen, who achieved 19 of his 80 with the triplane, Hans Kirschstein, who was credited with 16 of his 27 victories in the DrI and Werner Voss, with 10 of his 48. Of this quartet, only Jacobs survived the war.

## KNIGHTS OF THE AIR

### Josef Jacobs

Arguably the most diehard – and successful – Fokker DrI pilot, Josef Carl Peter Jacobs was born in Kreuzkapelle, Rhineland, on 15 May 1894. Learning to fly in 1912, he had served in the Luftstreitskräfte from the outbreak of war, and scored his first two victories in the spring of 1916 while flying in Fokker Staffel West. In November Jacobs transferred to Jagdstaffel 22 and also instructed at Jastaschule I through the winter of 1916-17. On 2 August 1917, Ltn Jacobs, with five victories, was given command of Jasta 7, with which unit he would raise his score to 12 by the end of the year. In early 1918 he received his first DrI, and became so enamoured with it that he would keep at least two on hand, even after acquiring one of the faster Fokker D.VIIs, until at least October 1918. Jacobs' stated means of overcoming the DrI's engine problems was to replace inoperative motors from a pool of British rotaries taken from downed Camels, often provided by front-line troops in return for a case of champagne! Jacobs' tally had been variously described as 44 or 48, more than 30 of those victories being scored in DrIs. Jacobs also survived two mid-air collisions, and was awarded the Orden Pour le Mérite on 18 July 1918.

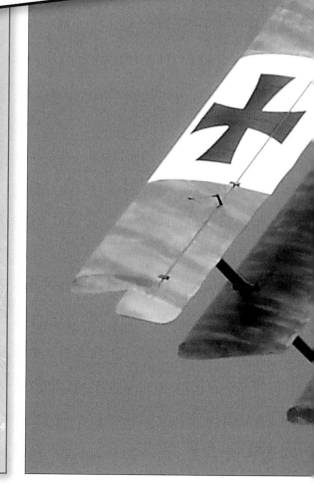

equip three newly formed Jagdgeschwadern (JGs I, II and III). However, production delays caused by the poor construction of the early DrIs stymied this plan. All triplanes in the front line were grounded for a month, and Fokker was forced to halt production while it provided strengthened wings for aircraft that had already been delivered. JG I's component Jasta slowly replaced their Albatros D.Vs and D.Vas as DrIs started leaving the Schwerin factory again in December 1917.

On 13 January 1918, Jasta 11 achieved the first aerial victory for the DrI when a British observation balloon was destroyed by Ltn Werner Steinhäuser. JGs II and III were established with the triplane in February 1918, and a handful of Jastas not assigned to these Jagdgeschwadern also received the DrI in varying quantities. The triplane reached its operational peak on the Western Front in April 1918 when 171 DrIs were in front-line service.

With the issuing of the superior Fokker D.VII to key Jagdgeschwadern from May 1918, the surviving DrIs were passed on to other Jastas. By the summer only Jasta 19 was fully equipped with the triplane. Even then, despite the DrI being obsolete when compared to the latest German and Allied fighter types, the aircraft was still preferred over second-rate Pfalz and Albatros machines, as Ltn Rudolf Stark of Jasta 34B confirmed: *'At last we too are going to get better machines – Fokker triplanes. It is true that they are discarded machines of the Jagdgeschwader (I), and therefore contain quite a lot of hidden snags, but that does not diminish our joy. Three of them have already turned up. There is great competition as to who is to fly them, and finally we let the dice decide'*.

The last operational DrIs were two aircraft assigned to Jasta 7 and flown exclusively by leading triplane ace Ltn Josef Jacobs. He was shot down by RAF SE5as while flying one of them in defence of Jasta 7's St Marguerite airfield on 3 October 1918.

*Right:* **Ltn Werner Steinhäuser of Jasta 11 swings the propeller on one of his own DrIs at Cappy in April 1918. Note the face on the aircraft's cowling.** *via Aviation-images.com*

*Bottom:* **Younger brother of the 'Red Baron', Ltn Lothar von Richthofen, crash-landed in DrI 454/17 after the leading edge of its top wing failed during combat with Bristol F2B Fighters of No 62 Squadron and Camels of No 73 Squadron on 13 March 1918.** *via Aviation-images.com*

# SURVIVORS

NO ORIGINAL Fokker DRIs have survived to this day. However, large number of replica DrIs have been built over the years with varying degrees of accuracy. In the UK, a Fokker DrI replica regularly takes to the air as part of the Great War Display Team, a popular airshow act designed to recreate the time of the knights of the sky. This replica was built by John Day in 2005/6, and it replicates 403/17 as flown by Leutnant Johann Janzen (13 victories) of Jasta 6, part of JG I. It carries the unit markings of a black/white striped tail and black cowling, with Janzen's well known personal marking of a 'white snake' line on a black band, edged in white around the rear fuselage.

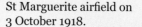

# FOKKER D.VII

**CREATED BY FOKKER'S** highly talented design team, the prototype D.VII was completed in great haste so that it could enter the German D-Type standard fighter competition in early 1918. Emerging the clear winner, it was put into widespread production by Fokker, as well as licensees Albatros and OAW. The D.VII proved to be one of the best scouts in service with either side. Proof of the fighter's formidable reputation came when the victorious Allies specifically stated in the surrender terms dictated to Germany that all surviving D.VIIs had to be handed over.

The Fokker D.VII is widely regarded as the finest German fighter aircraft of World War One and turned many of its pilots into aces. *Luigino Caliaro*

Although 1917 had dawned brightly for German fighter pilots with the success of the Albatros D.II and its successor the D.III during 'Bloody April', the year ended with uncertainty and frustration after the Allies introduced a succession of superb aircraft. The latter included France's sprightly 180hp SPAD VII and 220hp SPAD XIII and Britain's Bristol F2B Fighter, Royal Aircraft Factory SE5a, Sopwith Triplane and Sopwith Camel. German efforts to counter these machines with successors to the Albatros D.III during the latter half of 1917 and early 1918 were consistently met with disappointment.

Yet despite of the performance shortcomings of their fighters, German pilots managed to hold their own over the Western Front throughout this period thanks to their skill and the employment of superior tactics. They were also aided by the fact that they were fighting an essentially defensive war that saw Allied aircraft venturing over the frontline into German-held territory.

On 21 March 1918, however, Germany launched its final offensive of the war, Operation 'Michael'. At that time the Luftsteitskräfte's best available fighter was the Fokker DrI, yet less than 200 examples were available. Backing up the DrIs were Albatros D.Vs and D.Vas and Pfalz D.IIIs and D.IIIas, which were all desperately in need of replacement. In the weeks prior to the offensive commencing, pilots in the frontline had heard rumours that better aircraft would soon be reaching them, and examples of the Siemens-Schuckert Werke (SSW) D.III and the Fokker D.VII would begin to reach the Western Front in April.

These aircraft had been chosen for production by the Idflieg following a fighter competition held at Berlin's Adlershof airfield in late January 1918. No fewer than 31 contestants participated in the fly off, these aircraft being submitted by 10 manufacturers. Anthony Fokker had sent eight aircraft to Aldershof – the rotary-engined V9 biplane, the V11, V13 and V18 biplanes, the V17 and V20 monoplanes and two DrI triplanes. Although the stunning performance of the SSW D.III attracted most of the attention, it was Fokker's V11 and V18 that duly won the competition.

The former, heavily influenced by the DrI, featured a biplane version of its wooden box spar wing and was powered by the new high-compression straight-six Mercedes DIIIaü water-cooled engine. The lower wing, which was smaller than the upper in order to improve the pilot's downward visibility, was built in one piece and featured a cut-out in the steel tube fuselage frame to accommodate it. The ailerons, fitted to the upper wing only, were fabric covered steel tube, while the interplane and cabane struts were streamlined steel tubing. The V11 also featured a car-type radiator mounted in the nose.

Although ranking German ace Rittmeister Manfred Freiherr von Richthofen had been impressed by the V11's performance during early test flights, he told Fokker that it was directionally unstable and therefore prone to falling into a spin. The manufacturer duly responded by building a second machine that had a lengthened fuselage (increased by 40cm) and a vertical stabiliser added forward of the tail section. This aircraft was designated the V18. Both aircraft were tested at the January 1918 competition, where von Richthofen and his contemporaries pilots praised the biplane's performance. They were particularly impressed by its ability to retain its manoeuvrability at high altitude and to 'hang on its prop'.

The V21 was a final refinement on the V18, the aircraft featuring a smaller triangular vertical stabiliser. And it was this version of the new fighter that was ordered into production under the military designation D.VII. Fokker received a contract to build 400 fighters at a cost of 25,000 marks apiece. Such was the urgent demand for the new machine that Albatros' Johannisthal (Albatros) and Schneidemühl (Ostdeutsche Albatros Werke, or OAW) factories were ordered to manufacture the D.VII under license, with a five percent royalty going to Fokker.

D.VIIs began arriving at Jasta 10 of JG I in late April 1918.

Fokker-built D.VIIs of Saxon Jasta 72 show off their individual insignia in this impressive line-up on Bergnicourt aerodrome, near Rethel, north Reims, in July 1918. First in line is the distinctive 'M'-marked aircraft of Staffelführer Karl Menckhoff, who survived the war with 39 victories to his name – a large number of these claimed with the D.VII. *via Aviation-images.com*

WHEN THE FIRST examples of the Fokker D.VII reached the frontline, German fighter units were firmly on the back foot against their Allied opponents, who were flying better machines in greater numbers. Fortunately for the hard-pressed Jagdflieger, their new scout revealed levels of controllability that were to become legendary – indeed, standards against which all new fighters were to be adjudged for a decade or more after the war had ended. Admittedly, it was not the fastest or most manoeuvrable fighter over the Western Front in the summer and autumn of 1918, but it was undoubtedly the most effective.

The D.VII made use of some of the revolutionary structural features first seen in the DrI almost a year earlier, namely thick-section high-lift wings each built up on two wooden box-spars and dispensing with flying, landing and incidence wires. The fuselage, however, retained the typical Fokker wire-braced welded steel-tube primary structure.

One of the key features of the D.VII was its reworked Mercedes DIII engine, which had been installed in most German fighters from 1916 onward. The version developed for the Fokker fighter, however, was the IIIaü, which boasted higher compression that saw its 160hp soon increased to 180hp.

German fighter pilots immediately warmed to the inherent structural soundness of the D.VII. Ltn Fritz Friedrichs of Jasta 10 soon proved this when an exploding anti-aircraft shell broke a lower wing spar in half, but the overall wing cellule held together until he flew home. Many of the D.VII's virtues lay in its cantilever wing, whose thicker airfoil and high aspect ratio gave it a lift coefficient of 1.1, compared to 1.0 for its great rival the SPAD XIII, and consequently a superior rate of climb.

Once in service there seemed to be only three things wrong with the D.VII.

Elated though they were with the first examples of the fighter using the 180hp Mercedes IIIaü, many pilots thought it would benefit from a better engine – and later in 1918 it got two. Mercedes produced the 200hp IIIaüv, but it was the Fokker D.VIIf, powered by the 185hp BMW IIIa, that exhibited the best performance, especially at altitudes of 18,000ft or above.

A second more disturbing flaw was a tendency for the D.VII's ammunition to overheat and explode within the confines of its front cowling. On 15 July 1918, Fokker D.VII 309/18, flown by Ltn Fritz Friedrichs (Jasta 10's balloon specialist with 11 aeroplanes and 10 'gasbags' to his credit), suddenly burst into flame, most likely due to the spontaneous combustion of his phosphorus rounds. When his fuel tank exploded Friedrichs abandoned his aeroplane, but his parachute caught on the tailplane and ripped, causing the ace to plunge to his death. Improved ammunition eventually remedied this problem, but a common interim precaution was to cut ventilating holes or louvres in the cowling in a manner that varied between Jastas.

The D.VII's third, and arguably most vocally expressed, fault was that there never seemed to be enough of them to satisfy demand.

*Above:* **Zebra-striped D.VII 4598/18 of Jasta 5 was used by Ltn Josef Mai during the late summer of 1918, the ace claiming two of his 30 victories with the fighter. It had diagonal black/white stripes on the fuselage and tailplane as an attempt to throw off the aim of enemy airmen.** *via Aviation-images.com*

*Inset:* **This distinctively marked D.VII was assigned to 44-victory ace Hptm Bruno Loerzer, Kommandeur of JG III.** *via Aviation-images.com*

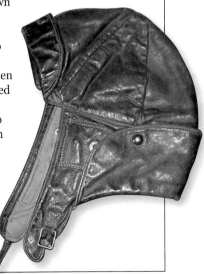

# FROM THE COCKPIT

REGARDED BY THOSE that flew it, and its foes, as the best all-round fighter of World War One, the D.VII earned this accolade by being a fairly easy, yet responsive, fighter to fly. It was forgiving, yet extraordinarily responsive; its stall was straightforward and it spun reluctantly. The fighter remained under full control when its adversaries stalled and spun, and it could 'hang on its propeller' at angles up to 45 degrees and remain a stable gun platform, allowing pilots to pepper their opponents from below with machine gun fire.

'The superiority of the British single-seat and reconnaissance aircraft makes it even more perceptibly unpleasant here. The single-seaters stay and fight after coming over at altitude. One cannot even shoot at them. Speed is the most important point. One could shoot down five to ten times as many if we were faster. Please give me news soon about when we can count on these new machines.' Von Richthofen was killed in action on 21 April – just days before his unit received production examples of the Fokker fighter.

## 'THE GERMAN FIGHTER HAS BECOME EQUAL TO THE BEST ENEMY SINGLE-SEATERS' Oblt Hermann Göring

The arrival of the D.VII in the frontline in the spring of 1918 was eagerly anticipated by the Jagdflieger, who were struggling to deal with vastly superior Allied aircraft types in their obsolete Albatros and Pfalz scouts and unreliable and increasingly rare DrIs. One of the leading proponents of the new Fokker scout was World War One's ranking ace, Rittmeister Manfred Freiherr von Richthofen, who had been harassing the high command of the German Army Air Service since March of that year. On 2 April he wrote the following note to his friend Oblt Fritz von Falkenhayn, the Kogenluft (Commander General of the air force) staff's technical officer: 'After a long time I come once again with a question. When can I count on the arrival of Fokker biplanes with the super-compressed engines?

The replacement of the DrI with the D.VII was immediately noted by the Allies on the Western Front, prompting the issuing of the following intelligence report to the SPAD-equipped American 1st Pursuit Group by the French VI Armeé, under whose auspices it was then serving, on 3 July 1918;

**Jasta 18's Vzfw Glatz and his D.VII at Montingen, near Metz, in northern France.**
*via Aviation-images.com*

'The triplane Fokker is disappearing little by little. The Fokker D.VII (biplane) is reported by our pursuit pilots to be encountered frequently. It is an excellent machine, being better than the 180hp SPAD and equal to the 220hp SPAD in horizontal speed, and it is apparently able to climb faster, is extremely manoeuvrable and able to continue acrobacy at high altitudes of 5,000 to 5,500 metres.'

Things only got worse for the Allies with the introduction of the 185hp BMW IIIa-engined D.VIIf from mid-1918. This combination quickly made the fighter the terror of the Western Front, as Ltn Wenzl recalled: 'On 22 June the first BMW Fokkers arrived and were issued to Jasta 11. The aces each got one as well. I led the Staffel while Kirschstein was in Berlin, and I tried out his BMW, which pleased me greatly. This machine easily reached 6,000 metres in 24 minutes – that was a tremendous feat in those days. The effects of these new machines immediately became evident. Staffel 11 was once more shooting down a good many machines.'

Such was the increase in performance of the BMW Fokkers that everyone was keen to get them as quickly as possible. One such individual was Oblt Hermann Göring, the final Kommandeur of JG I, who noted in one of his technical reports: 'By production and introduction of the BMW IIIa motor, the German fighter has become equal, or frequently superior, to the best enemy single-seaters. This high altitude motor is a great advancement over all past motors. Each fighter pilot urgently requires a BMW motor.'

One of the pilots to make the best use of the D.VIIf was Jasta 4's high-scoring ace Ltn Ernst Udet, who saw much action in the final months of the war: 'I noticed more than ever during this period how much of a performance advantage I enjoyed in my BMW-engined fighter over the other Mercedes-engined machines of my Staffel I gave a second BMW machine to Ltn Heinrich Drekmann, and we carried out many patrols together. We now used to cross the lines at a height of 5,900 metres, which had not been possible with other engines, and we could stay at this altitude six to twelve miles behind the enemy lines without being spotted. Our fights began mostly with surprise attacks, giving us tactical advantage that usually resulted in victory.'

## LÖWENHARDT

The legendary yellow Fokker D.VII of Oblt Erich Löwenhardt, Germany's third ranking ace of World War One, behind only Manfred von Richthofen and Ernst Udet. Löwenhardt was an aggressive, skilled fighter whose score grew steadily. At the end of May 1918 he received Germany's highest honour, the Pour le Mérite (Blue Max) after 24 kills. Flying the new Fokker D.VII, he added eight more in June and no fewer than 16 in July. His tally climbed to 53 on 9 August. After scoring his 54th victory, he collided with Ltn Alfred Wenz of Jasta 11. Both men jumped from their planes but Löwenhardt was killed when his parachute failed to open and he fell to his death from 12,000ft. *Painting by Russell Smith*

## FACT FILE

## CONSTRUCTION

### COCKPIT

The cockpit of the D.VII was very similar to preceding D-series scouts built by German manufacturers. The fighter's cockpit featured three key instruments, namely a tachometer and main and auxiliary fuel tank pressure gauges. Nestled between the 'Spandau' guns at eye level was the fuel gauge, while a compass was fitted to the right of the pilot's bucket seat. He had a tubular steel control column and a rudder control bar.

### FUSELAGE

The fuselage was a braced box-girder welded from thin-walled mild-steel tube in the traditional Fokker manner. These were internally rigged with single strands of piano wire to give it structural strength. Forward of the cockpit the structure became more complex, so as to provide adequate strength to support the engine. Metal panels covered the fuselage sides back to the leading edge of the lower wing and back to the cockpit on the top decking.

### TAIL

The D.VII's characteristic triangular tailplane and fin were fabricated from light-gauge steel tube and covered in fabric.

### WINGS

The thick-section high-lift cantilever wings were each built up on two wooden box-spars that tapered in depth towards the tips. The D.VII featured a 'one-piece' lower wing, this being accommodated by a special cut-out in the lower longerons.

### ARMAMENT

The D.VII was armed with two synchronised 7.92mm LMG 08/15 'Spandau' machine guns. The aircraft carried 1,000 rounds of ammunition in boxes immediately below the weapons and forward of the cockpit. The machine gun butts protruded into the cockpit at near eye level, and the pilot aimed these weapons using a ring-and-bead sight at the very end of the weapons.

### UNDERCARRIAGE

The fixed undercarriage was of conventional design for the period, consisting of streamline section steel-tube vee struts that were attached to the aircraft via sockets welded to the lower fuselage.

### ENGINE

Initially, the D.VII was fitted with 160hp version of Mercedes' trusty six-cylinder DIII inline water-cooled engine. This was soon replaced by the higher-compression DIIIaü version, which produced 180hp at higher altitudes, and the DIIIaüv of 200hp. However, it was the Fokker D.VIIf, powered by the all-new 185hp BMW IIIa, that exhibited the best performance, especially at altitudes of 18,000ft or above.

**1917**

**December:**
The first of two prototype Fokker V11s, from which the D.VII was derived, completes its maiden flight in December 1917.

**1918**

**January:**
Fokker V11 and V18 win fighter competition at Adlershof, earning acceptance for production as the D.VII.

**April:**
First Fokker D.VIIs arrive JG I's Jasta 10

via Aviation-images.com

Geschwader-Stock in his right hand, Oblt Göring poses proudly in front of his immaculate D.VIIf 5125/18. By the time this photograph was taken in late September 1918 Göring had claimed his 22nd, and last, victory.

**May:**
Erich Löwenhardt of ta 10 credited with first kker D.VII victory, an 5a, followed by a DH 9 e next evening.

**September:**
JG III is credited with 130 victories over RAF aircraft in September after the Geschwader is issued with BMW-engined D.VIIfs.

**6 November:**
Fokker D.VII pilots of JG I claim three SPAD XIIIs for the 'Flying Circus" last victories of World War One.

**11 November:**
The Armistice brings an end to World War One.

**28 June:**
Signing of Treaty of Versailles, which includes a specific clause demanding surrender of all D.VIIs to the Allies.

Fokker D.VII (OAW) 4453/18 of Ltn Alfred Lindenberger, Jasta 'Boelcke', Aniche, France, November 1918

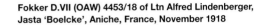

*Luigino Caliaro*

## SPECIFICATIONS

### Fokker D.VIIf

| | |
|---|---|
| Engine: | BMW IIIa |
| Power: | 185hp |
| Max Speed: | 125mph (200km/h) |
| Length: | 22ft 9.7in (6.95m) |
| Wing span: | 29ft 2.3in (8.90m) |
| Height: | 9ft 2.25in (2.75m) |
| Armament: | Two 7.92mm Maxim LMG 08/15 'Spandau' machine guns |
| Max all-up weight: | 2,006lb (910kg) |
| Range: | Endurance of 1.5 hours |

**IN CLOSE-UP**

*Luigino Caliaro*

## DID YOU KNOW?

● The Fokker D.VII was yet another fighting scout created by the company's designer, Reinhold Platz, who had been responsible for the iconic DrI triplane of 1917.

● Although Rittmeister Manfred Freiherr von Richthofen had avidly looked forward to flying the D.VII in combat himself (indeed, he influenced the refinement of its design after test flying the V11), he was killed in action on 21 April – just days before his unit received production examples of the fighter.

● So formidable was the D.VII that it was specifically named by type in the list of items to be handed over to the victorious Allies following the Armistice in November 1918.

● Precise production figures for the D.VII have been lost, but it is thought that 3,200 were ordered and 1,720+ delivered before the Armistice.

# IN COMBAT

PRODUCTION EXAMPLES of the D.VII were collected by Jagdgeschwader I's Jasta 10 in late April 1918 and flown to the unit's airfield at Beugneux. JG I, better known as 'Richthofen's Circus', had been formed in June 1917 as a permanent grouping of four Jagdstaffeln (Jastas 4, 6, 10 and 11) that would from now on operate as a unit. As such, it was sent to various fronts to support a specific battle area.

Aside from JG I, JGs II (Jastas 12, 13, 15 and 19) and III (Jastas 2, 26, 27 and 36) were fully equipped with D.VIIs by early July 1918 – a total of 407 aircraft were in service with the three Jagdgeschwader at this point in the conflict. Independent army Jastas and naval Marine Feld Jastas also began to receive Fokker fighters from the late summer through to war's end too, by which time 775 D.VIIs were in frontline service.

JG I gave the fighter its operational debut just as Germany's 'Michael' offensive was about to enter its third phase. By now the element of surprise and much of the offensive's initiative had been lost, which meant that the tactical deployment of the Jagdgeschwader reverted

OAW D.VII 4071/18 of Kest 4b appears to have either ground-looped on landing or suffered engine failure on take off at Freiburg, in Germany. Despite the destruction the pilot, Vzfw Buder, was able to walk away from the wreckage.
*via Aviation-images.com*

Individually marked D.VIIs from various units occupy Nivelles airfield, in Belgium, shortly after the Armistice in November 1918. The D.VII in the foreground is marked with the broad black and white stripes of JG III's Jasta 26. *via Aviation-images.com*

## ACES

With the ability to turn a mediocre pilot into a good one and a good pilot into an ace, the D.VII was always destined to have an impact on aerial combat over the Western Front in the final seven months of the war. Close to 50 Jastas would eventually be equipped with the Fokker fighter, with aces flying these aircraft along the entire Western Front from the North Sea coast to the Swiss border. Not only the mainstay of the army Jagdstaffeln, the D.VII was also the most potent fighter flown by home defence Kests and the pilots of the German navy in Flanders. Amongst the leading D.VII aces were Erich Löwenhardt, Ernst Udet, Lothar von Richthofen, Rudolph Berthold, Franz Büchner, Bruno Loerzer, and Paul Bäumer, all amassing individual totals in excess of 40 victories.

to the situation prior to Operation 'Michael'. Units were now being shifted from one base to another to concentrate against whichever Allied offensive seemed most threatening at the time. One such clash took place during the final German offensive along the Marne from 14 July 1918, when all three Jagdgeschwader and other crack Fokker D.VII-equipped Jastas fought the most seasoned Groupe de Combat and escadrilles of French Escadre I, as well as the American 1st Pursuit Group.

In spite of the flagging spirits permeating the German army following the failure of 'Michael', the D.VII pilots retained faith in their aeroplanes and a dogged determination to do their part in making the Allies pay dearly for every gain, on the ground or in the air. Given the overwhelming and still growing preponderance of aircraft swelling the Allied ranks, however, the D.VII pilots could do little more than delay their country's ultimate, inevitable defeat. The odds facing them at this time were perfectly summed up by ace Ltn Alfred Wenz of Jasta 11: *'It was necessary to take off on patrols three to five times a day, which meant that daily we had flyers who were killed, wounded or missing in action. In the last months of the war, we would have 20 or 30 aircraft in the air at one time, and it was necessary that we combat the American, English or French groups of 100 to 120 aeroplanes'.*

# KNIGHTS OF THE AIR

## Georg von Hantelmann

Georg von Hantelmann was born in Rokietnice (which is now part of Poland) on 9 October 1898. He joined the German Army in 1916, and was soon commissioned into the Braunschweiger Hussar Regiment Nr 17 – (the unit's Death's Head insignia would decorate his various fighters in the frontline). Transferring to air service a short while later, von Hantelmann joined Jasta 15 on 18 March 1918 and recorded his first success on 6 June – by month-end his tally stood at four victories confirmed and three unconfirmed.

Issued with a Fokker D.VII in July 1918, von Hantelmann's score then began to rapidly increase. Two victories came in August, then 12 during September, seven more in October and his 25th, and last, on 4 November. Amongst von Hantelmann's victims were American aces 1Lts David Putnam (13 victories) and Joseph Wehner (six victories) and French ace Sous-Lt Maurice Boyau (35 victories).

Surviving the war, having just turned 20, von Hantelmann was fated to die at the hands of Polish poachers on his estate in East Prussia on 7 September 1924.

A youthful Ltn Georg von Hantelmann poses alongside his D.VII, which has been adorned with a wreath to mark his 20th victory. The photograph was taken at Charmois aerodrome on 9 October 1918. *via Aviation-images.com*

Such odds led to some outstanding scores by German pilots, who were never short of opponents when aloft. Men such as Ernst Udet and Paul Baümer cut a swathe through Allied formations, the latter pilot's parent unit, JG III, being credited with 130 victories over RAF aircraft in September 1918 alone after the Geschwader had been issued with BMW-engined D.VIIfs. Baümer was credited with 16 of them, taking his tally from 22 to 38 victories – he would finish the war with a score of 43.

The D.VII allowed the German fighter force to remain a constant threat to Allied air operations right up until the Armistice brought an end to World War One. Indeed, these agile machines, although only available in modest numbers, wrought much havoc on the Western Front – the sight of 'straight wings' approaching in a stepped-up gaggle struck anxiety and fear into many a stout-hearted Allied pilot.

Such was the regard of the Allied Powers for the capabilities of the D.VII that it was specifically singled out for mention in the Armistice Agreement article, which designated items that were to be handed over to the Allies 'In erster Linie alle apparate D.VII' ('especially all first-line D.VII aircraft').

*Surrounded by RAF pilots, at least two of which are in full flying gear, a captured D.VII from Jasta 27 provides the backdrop for this photograph taken at war's end at the Nivelles collection centre.*
*via Aviation-images.com*

# SURVIVORS

THE FACT THAT the D.VII was present in significant numbers when the Armistice came into effect, and subsequently remained in production in Holland thanks to the smuggling of complete, but dismantled, airframes from Germany at war's end, has meant that a handful of examples have survived into the 21st century. Indeed, no fewer than seven aircraft can be seen on display in Europe or North America.

One of the most authentic specimens is Albatros-built 6810/18, which has been maintained by the Brome County Historical Society of Knowlton, Quebec, since 1920. It is the sole survivor of 22 D.VIIs shipped to Canada as war trophies in 1919, these aircraft being passed on to various universities. It still retains much of its original five-colour lozenge fabric.

The RAF Museum's Albatros-built D.VII 8417/18 was captured by the Allies in Ostend after it was abandoned by a retreating Jasta 71 in October 1918. Stored in France until brought to England by R. G. Nash in 1938, the fighter was acquired by the Royal Aeronautical Society after World War Two. The subject of an immaculate four-year restoration at Cardington, the D.VII was put back on display in its Hendon home in 1997 finished in an authentic five-colour lozenge scheme.

*The sole D.VII in France, Albatros-built 6796/18, currently hangs in Le Grand Gallerie within the Le Bourget-based Musée de l'Air. One of many war prizes seized by the French in November 1918, it has been displayed in the museum ever since.*

## REPLICAS

Aside from the original airframes, at least 14 D.VII replicas are currently in existence worldwide, some of which include original parts in their airframes. A handful of the replicas are also airworthy flyers, being powered by period Mercedes DIII engines.